Introduction

The September 11, 2001, terrorist attacks resulted in nearly 3,000 deaths and roughly $44 billion of insured losses (in 2014 dollars). In light of the unexpected and unprecedented losses from the attacks, as well as the heightened uncertainty surrounding future losses, private insurers subsequently sharply reduced the availability of terrorism coverage for businesses and commercial properties. Policymakers were concerned that without terrorism insurance, financing for commercial development projects in high-risk areas would be unavailable and that new construction and job creation would be reduced, thereby slowing economic growth. (Estimating how large those effects would have been is difficult, in part because some construction and job creation would probably have shifted to lower-risk areas; such shifts might have reduced losses in the event of future attacks.)

In response, lawmakers enacted the Terrorism Risk Insurance Act (TRIA) in 2002 as a temporary measure to provide catastrophic federal reinsurance for terrorism risk without charging premiums up front. Although no major terrorist attacks have occurred in the United States since 9/11 and thus the government has paid no claims, the threat of terrorist attacks persists. Lawmakers reauthorized TRIA in 2005 and 2007 and again in January 2015 for six years, just days after the program lapsed at the end of 2014. The law requires primary insurers to offer terrorism coverage on business and commercial policies (including workers' compensation insurance). By coupling that requirement with a federal reinsurance program, which protects insurers against large losses, TRIA helps to ensure the availability of insurance coverage and might reduce insurers' insolvencies and economic disruption after a large terrorist attack. But, as structured, the program exposes the government to a significant amount of financial risk and subsidizes policyholders (many of which are large businesses).

Before TRIA was reauthorized in 2015, the Congressional Budget Office produced a brief analysis of the effects of the previous program and its expiration, as well as various options for reinstating or revising it.[1] This working paper supplements that report by providing more background on terrorism risk and the federal response to that risk and examining in more detail some policy options that might be considered in the future. Specifically, this paper discusses the potential effects of increasing the extent of the risk borne by private insurers and policyholders (by changing terms of the TRIA contracts or limiting the program to attacks using nonconventional weapons), charging risk-based prices for federal coverage, and changing the tax code to encourage the private provision of terrorism insurance.

Terrorism Risk

The terrorist attacks of September 11, 2001, inflicted very large personal and commercial property damage, much of which was insured. Insurers responded by sharply limiting the availability of coverage or pricing it at elevated rates that made coverage in high-risk areas unattractive to most potential purchasers; those responses reduced risk sharing and had the potential to slow commercial construction and to reduce economic activity. The federal government responded to the losses—insured and uninsured—in part by providing compensation to families of the victims and by providing funds to aid New York City's economic and physical redevelopment.

Although there have been no other major terrorist attacks that resulted in large property losses in the United States since September 11, the possibility of such attacks remains a concern. Despite

---

[1] Congressional Budget Office, *Federal Reinsurance for Terrorism Risk: An Update* (January 2015), www.cbo.gov/publication/49866. That paper updated the analysis in Congressional Budget Office, *Federal Reinsurance for Terrorism Risks: Issues in Reauthorization* (August 2007), www.cbo.gov/publication/19035.

improvements in the modeling of terrorism risk, the frequency and severity of catastrophic attacks—which depend not on natural forces subject to physical laws, but on strategic choices by terrorists and the effectiveness of counterterrorism efforts—remain particularly uncertain, leading insurers to limit the amount of capital they put at risk.

The broad arguments for and against government intervention in the terrorism insurance market shed light on current policy and on possible future changes. Government intervention can increase the availability of coverage and spread risks more widely, increase economic activity in areas of greatest risk before any attack, and, after an attack, reduce demands for assistance and help stabilize the economy. However, intervention subsidizes policyholders, especially those in high-risk areas, and thus discourages the mitigation of risk, increases the government's exposure, and limits opportunities for sharing risk more broadly with the private sector domestically and abroad. Whether the balance of those effects is likely to be positive or negative for the economy depends on several factors, including the accuracy of private and governmental perceptions of risk and the extent to which insurance coverage has spillover benefits or costs.

The Attacks of September 11, 2001

The terrorist attacks of September 11 in New York City, Washington, D.C., and Pennsylvania killed nearly 3,000 people and resulted in insurance payments from private insurers of about $32.5 billion ($44 billion in 2014 dollars) for life, aviation, property, business interruption, workers' compensation, and other covered losses.[2] (Workers' compensation insurance provides wage replacement and medical benefits to employees who are injured on the job, as well as death benefits to survivors of workers who die in a work-related accident. The benefits are paid regardless of the cause of the injury or death, and regardless of who would be considered at fault.) Only Hurricane Katrina has caused greater insured losses in the United States. The largest share of the insured losses from the 9/11 attacks was covered by property and casualty insurers; their policies covered the damages to commercial buildings, motor vehicles, and business equipment and the loss of personal income through workers' compensation insurance and business income. Global reinsurance companies—private firms that agree to share portions of the risks in policies generated by other insurers in return for premiums—covered the majority of the losses. But after the 9/11 attacks, reinsurers virtually stopped writing new coverage, which shifted all the catastrophic risk back to the primary insurers.

Insurers' Reactions. After large and unexpected losses, such as those from natural catastrophes, insurance markets often experience disruption, with large and abrupt reductions in supply and changes in terms of coverage. Those effects typically diminish over time as insurers adjust their prices to account for changes to the perceived risks.[3] In the case of the 9/11 terrorist attacks, large short-term effects occurred as the result of several factors:

- The large losses lowered insurers' capital, which temporarily reduced their willingness and ability to bear risk.

- Insurers had underestimated the potential for losses from terrorism, and their estimates of future losses from terrorist attacks were uncertain. They had little information on which to base their understanding of either the frequency of attacks or the potential losses from attacks.

---

[2] Robert P. Hartwig and Claire Wilkinson, *Terrorism Risk: A Constant Threat 2014* (white paper, Insurance Information Institute, March 2014), www.iii.org/white-paper/terrorism-risk-a-constant-threat-2014-032114.

[3] Kenneth A. Froot, "The Intermediation of Financial Risks: Evolution in the Catastrophe Reinsurance Market," *Risk Management and Insurance Review*, vol. 11, no. 2 (Fall 2008), pp. 281–294.

Consequently, they were less willing to risk their capital by covering terrorism risk. The sharp contraction in the availability of reinsurance limited primary insurers' ability to diversify their risk of catastrophic losses.

- Insurers realized that large terrorism attacks carry significant market risk.[4] Because global stock prices declined after 9/11 and the economy weakened, the value of insurers' assets fell at the same time that they faced large claims. Shareholders require additional compensation to bear market risk; that factor, along with the uncertainty surrounding risk estimates, contributed to insurers' decisions to charge significantly higher prices for terrorism coverage.

Before 9/11, insurers generally covered losses from terrorist attacks using conventional weapons but did not explicitly charge for that risk, implicitly treating it as if it were negligible.[5] They did so even though the 9/11 attacks were not the first in the United States. (The April 1995 bombing of the federal building in Oklahoma City killed 168 people and resulted in nearly $200 million of insured property and casualty losses, measured in 2014 dollars. In addition, the February 26, 1993, bombings in the garage of the World Trade Center killed six people and resulted in nearly $840 million in insured property and casualty losses, measured in 2014 dollars.)

After 9/11 and before the enactment of TRIA in November 2002, insurers generally either charged much higher prices for terrorism coverage or attempted to exclude it altogether. In some cases, however, state regulations prevented insurers from excluding terrorism risk. For example, after 9/11, five states, including New York and California, required terrorism insurance to be included in commercial property and casualty insurance. In many other states, property insurance already covered losses from fire regardless of cause. Moreover, nearly all states required employers to provide workers' compensation policies, which do not exclude losses caused by nuclear, biological, chemical, and radiological (NBCR) attacks and do not cap insurers' liabilities, and most states regulated the rates for workers' compensation coverage. Thus, insurers had less ability to adjust coverage terms or rates than they did for property insurance, as remains the case today.

Federal Assistance. In addition to private insurance, federal assistance to individuals, businesses, and state and local governments following the 9/11 attacks totaled at least $33 billion (depending on which outlays are assumed to be in response to the attacks), but only a fraction of that amount went to uninsured businesses.[6] Just over $20 billion of the assistance was targeted to the New York City area—$15.7 billion

---

[4] Market risk is one component of financial risk: It is the component that remains even after a portfolio has been diversified as much as possible. Investors tend to demand additional compensation, called a market risk premium, to hold assets that perform relatively poorly when the economy is weak and relatively well when the economy is strong. People value income from investments more when the economy is weak and incomes are relatively low and so assign a higher cost to losses that occur during economic downturns. Similarly, insurers must pay their investors a market risk premium to support coverage of risks that can result in large payoffs when the economy is weak. Large terrorist attacks carry market risk, in part because they can affect the outlook for investment. The same is true for some catastrophic natural disasters, such as the 2011 earthquake and tsunami that devastated parts of Japan and led to nuclear accidents. In that case, to stabilize financial markets, the Bank of Japan eased monetary policy and provided funds sufficient to meet the needs of financial markets.

[5] In contrast, losses from attacks involving nuclear, biological, chemical, and radiological weapons were excluded from coverage under most lines of insurance other than workers' compensation. Howard C. Kunreuther, Mark V. Pauly, and Stacey McMorrow, *Insurance and Behavioral Economics* (Cambridge University Press, 2013), pp. 162–184, www.cambridge.org/us/academic/subjects/economics/industrial-economics/insurance-and-behavioral-economics-improving-decisions-most-misunderstood-industry?format=PB.

[6] The estimates, which have not been adjusted for inflation, also vary depending on the source. For more details, see Congressional Budget Office, *Federal Terrorism Reinsurance: An Update* (January 2005), pp. 25–26, www.cbo.gov/publication/16210; and letter from Dan L. Crippen, Director, Congressional Budget Office, to the Honorable Carolyn B. Maloney, U.S. House of Representatives, October 29, 2002, ww12w.cbo.gov/publication/14194.

in direct spending and \$5 billion in tax benefits. Most of that assistance, however, went to efforts to respond to the initial emergencies, to remove debris, and to restore public infrastructure. (The rest of the \$33 billion included \$7 billion paid to victims or their relatives from the September 11th Victim Compensation Fund and \$5 billion paid to U.S. airlines as compensation for losses sustained as a direct result of the terrorist attacks.)

Most of the aid was authorized through three emergency supplemental appropriation acts dealing with recovery from and response to terrorist attacks (Public Laws 107-38, 107-117, and 107-206). Aid after a disaster is often designated as emergency spending, not subject to such standard budgetary rules as the annual limits placed on overall discretionary spending or the amounts allocated to each appropriations subcommittee.[7]

Current Risks

No large-scale attacks on properties have occurred in the United States since 9/11, but the United States, like other countries, faces persistent international and domestic terrorist threats, according to national security analysts.[8] One reason for the absence of such attacks is that counterterrorism policies and surveillance have disrupted terrorist organizations and cells, as well as numerous plots.[9] Another reason is that attacks on the scale of 9/11 are difficult to carry out. For example, although some plots in the United States were not detected ahead of time, they still failed for operational reasons. That was the case for the attempted aircraft bombings in December 2009 and May 2012 and for a Times Square car bomb in May 2010. None of those attacks would have come close to the scale of the September 11 attacks.

But some attacks have occurred—notably the April 2013 bombings at the Boston Marathon, which killed three people and left more than 250 injured—and they can be expected to recur in the future. (Insured property and casualty losses from the Boston Marathon attack were too small to trigger coverage under TRIA—indeed, they were below even the minimum threshold of \$5 million of insured property and casualty losses required for an attack to be certified as a "terrorist act" by the Secretary of the Treasury, who is responsible for doing so under the law.)

Modeling terrorism risk is very difficult, and modelers' estimates of expected losses are highly uncertain and may change quickly. The set of known attacks on which to base an analysis is relatively small. Moreover, past attacks may be of limited relevance because governments institute countermeasures and terrorists change their tactics. The new counterterrorism campaign against ISIL (the Islamic State of Iraq and the Levant), a jihadist terrorist group operating largely in Iraq and Syria, illustrates how quickly

---

[7] Peterson-Pew Commission on Budget Reform, *Budgeting for Emergencies* (December 13, 2011), http://budgetreform.org/document/budgeting-emergencies.

[8] See the testimonies of James B. Comey, Director of the Federal Bureau of Investigation, Matthew G. Olsen, Director of the National Counterterrorism Center, and Rand Beers, Acting Secretary of the Department of Homeland Security, before the Senate Committee on Homeland Security and Governmental Affairs (November 14, 2013), www.hsgac.senate.gov/hearings/threats-to-the-homeland.

[9] On the basis of publicly available data, more is known about federal spending on counterterrorism policies (primarily for border and transportation security) than on spending by state and local governments. Very little is known about private-sector spending to reduce losses from terrorist attacks. See Office of Management and Budget, *Budget of the U.S. Government, Fiscal year 2016: Analytical Perspectives* (February 2016), pp. 341–349, www.whitehouse.gov/omb/budget/Analytical_Perspectives. For analysis of the effects of counterterrorism policies, see Henry H. Willis and Omar Al-Shahery, *National Security Perspectives on Terrorism Risk Insurance in the United States* (Policy Brief, RAND Center for Catastrophic Risk Management and Compensation, March 6, 2014), www.rand.org/pubs/research_reports/RR573.html; and testimony of Seth G. Jones, RAND, *The Extremist Threat to the U.S. Homeland,* before the House Homeland Security Committee (January 15, 2014), www.Rand.org/pubs/testimonies/CT403.html.

potential threat assessments can change.[10] Future attacks might not be limited to explosives or to the use of commercial aircraft as weapons. In particular, NBCR weapons might be used in future attacks, and at least some of the losses from such attacks would be covered by primary insurers and thereby by TRIA. By some estimates, a nuclear attack could result in losses of hundreds of billions of dollars (particularly in the workers' compensation line) and thousands of lives.[11] In addition, cyber-based threats (such as those associated with deliberate interruptions of computer systems, payment systems, and the power grid) may have increased in recent years. (Those threats are covered by some property and casualty policies and thus by TRIA.) Most of those threats, however, have come from criminals and state-sponsored groups rather than terrorists.

Modelers of terrorism risk have generally lowered their estimates of expected annual losses from terrorist attacks in recent years.[12] Those estimates of expected losses are now a few billion dollars a year or less, which is small compared with estimates of expected losses from natural disasters, such as hurricanes and earthquakes.[13] However, those estimates of losses from terrorist attacks are sensitive to the expected frequency of large attacks and could be several times larger or much smaller if those expectations changed.

Is There a Federal Role in Insuring Terrorism Risk?

The major rationale for government intervention in the terrorism insurance market is to promote more risk sharing than would occur in a purely private market and to avoid gaps in coverage that could occur after future terrorist attacks. Those coverage gaps could be short term if private reinsurers pulled back significantly from the market or greatly increased their prices, or they could be longer term if the limited information available about terrorism risk kept reinsurance prices inefficiently high. But federal intervention to address such gaps and increase risk sharing might have the unintended consequence of increasing the losses from terrorist attacks.

---

[10] White House, "Statement by the President on ISIL" (remarks, September 10, 2014), www.whitehouse.gov/the-press-office/2014/09/10/remarks-president-barack-obama-address-nation.

[11] Radiological, biological, and chemical attacks would probably result in smaller losses. See Peter Chalk and others, *Trends in Terrorism: Threats to the United States and the Future of the Terrorism Risk Insurance Act* (RAND Center for Terrorism Risk Management Policy, 2005), www.rand.org/pubs/monographs/MG393.html; and Lloyd Dixon and others, *The Federal Role in Terrorism Insurance: Evaluating Alternatives in an Uncertain World* (RAND Center for Terrorism Risk Management Policy, 2007), www.rand.org/pubs/monographs/MG679.html.

[12] The modelers take into account the effectiveness of counterterrorism policies and generally place low estimates on the probability of another 9/11-size attack and very low estimates of a major attack using NBCR weapons. See Gordon Woo, *Understanding the Principles of Terrorism Risk Modeling From the Charlie Hebdo Attack in Paris* (Risk Management Solutions, January 26, 2015), www.rms.com/blog/2015/01/26/paris-in-the-winter-assessing-terrorism-risk-after-charlie-hebdo/; testimony of Gordon Woo, Risk Management Solutions, before the House Committee on Financial Services (September 19, 2013), http://financialservices.house.gov/uploadedfiles/hhrg-113-ba00-wstate-gwoo-20130919.pdf (913 KB); Risk Management Solutions, *Quantifying U.S. Terrorism Risk* (white paper, December 2013), www.rms.com/resources/publications/terrorism; and Gary Ackerman and William C. Potter, "Catastrophic Nuclear Terrorism: A Preventable Peril," in Nick Bostrom and Milan M. Cirkovic, eds., *Global Catastrophic Risks* (Oxford University Press, 2008), pp. 402–449, http://global.oup.com/academic/product/global-catastrophic-risks-9780198570509?cc=us&lang=en&. At least one modeling firm has not reduced its estimates, however; see Thomas Mount, Michael Russo, and Andrew Colannino, *The Treatment of Terrorism Risk in the Rating Evaluation* (A.M. Best Methodology, November 27, 2013); www3.ambest.com/ambv/ratingmethodology/OpenPDF.aspx?rc=197680. For background on NBCR terrorism risk, see Graham Allison, *Nuclear Terrorism: The Ultimate Preventable Catastrophe* (Times Books and Henry Holt & Co., 2004), http://us.macmillan.com/books/9780805078527.

[13] Over the past 10 years, losses from natural disasters in the United States have averaged more than $25 billion a year (in 2013 dollars). See Insurance Information Institute, *Catastrophes: Insurance Issues* (August 2014), www.iii.org/issue-update/catastrophes-insurance-issues.

Arguments For Federal Involvement. Without government involvement, the private market for terrorism insurance might not maximize the gains to society if the risk perceptions of insurers or potential policyholders are systematically less accurate than the government's, or if insurance coverage has value to society in addition to its value to individual policyholders.[14] Those factors have different implications as to whether the government's involvement should merely strive to ensure a supply of insurance or also include subsidies to increase purchases:

- If insurers overestimate risks—for example, if they overcompensate in adjusting their expectations after a major attack—then the government may be able to improve economic efficiency by selling insurance or reinsurance at unsubsidized prices (those that reflect the estimated risk exposures of the insured properties).

- If potential policyholders misperceive risks, federal subsidies for insurance coverage may improve or reduce efficiency, depending on the nature of the misperceptions and the degree to which policyholders regard coverage as a substitute for mitigation.

- If insurance coverage has social benefits separate from its private benefits, the larger those social benefits, the stronger the argument for subsidies.

Limited information about terrorism risk may lead insurers to overestimate that risk, in which case they may set premiums very high, ration coverage, or not offer coverage at all.[15] Such misperceptions could be costly to the economy before an attack, but much more so after a successful large attack, which could deplete much of the capital that helps insurers fund all of their insurance risks, not just terrorism risk.[16] In that case, if investors were unwilling to supply sufficient inflows of new capital, the risk of widespread insolvencies among insurers would reduce the availability of terrorism coverage and possibly also other types of property and casualty coverage. In turn, the limited availability of terrorism insurance might hamper growth. Investors might shy away from putting up capital and, consequently, developers might delay or drop new commercial construction projects in major urban areas that otherwise would be undertaken. Moreover, in the absence of insurance coverage, businesses would be slower to recover after experiencing losses from terrorism.

Insurers' misperceptions that significantly reduced the availability of terrorism coverage after an attack would also be costly to the federal government. Reduced economic activity would lead to reductions in tax revenues; in addition, businesses without terrorism insurance would have greater tax deductions for uninsured losses and would be more likely to seek disaster assistance from the government (although most such assistance goes to state and local governments and to individuals, not to businesses).

---

[14] The private market for insurance in general has an important limitation in that claims on an insolvent insurer cannot be enforced. That limitation underpins capital requirements imposed by state regulators to ensure that policies meet a certain level of reliability, as well as state guaranty funds that spread the costs of insolvencies after they occur. (Guaranty funds cover the residential, automobile, and workers' compensation claims on insolvent insurers; coverage for most commercial lines of insurance is effectively limited. See Insurance Information Institute, *Insolvencies/Guaranty Funds* (issue update, September 2014), www.iii.org/issue-update/insolvencies-guaranty-funds.) The federal government is also likely to be involved in the event of widespread insolvencies after a catastrophic natural disaster or terrorist attack, serving as the insurer of last resort, although the cap on liability under TRIA attempts to limit that role. The questions addressed in the text focus on possible additional federal roles in the market for terrorism insurance specifically.

[15] For additional analysis, see Congressional Budget Office, *Federal Reinsurance for Disasters* (September 2002), pp. 2–4 and 19–21, www.cbo.gov/publication/14008.

[16] Robert E. Litan, "Sharing and Reducing the Financial Risks of Future 'Mega-Catastrophes,'" *Issues in Economic Policy*, no. 4 (Brookings Institution, March 2006), www.brookings.edu/research/papers/2006/03/business-litan02.

Potential buyers of terrorism insurance may also misperceive terrorism risk. If they underestimate the risk, they are likely to buy less coverage (so the risk would not be spread as widely as it could be) and to underinvest in mitigation. Alternatively, if they overestimate the risk—for example, because they lack information about government efforts to prevent future attacks—they may buy more coverage than they need, overinvest in mitigation, or both. If such misperceptions are common, government subsidies for terrorism coverage might increase economic efficiency in two ways: If businesses that underestimate the risk do not see insurance coverage as a close substitute for mitigation, then subsidies may improve efficiency by encouraging more risk spreading through insurance without undermining incentives for mitigation; conversely, if businesses that overestimate the risk see coverage as a close substitute for mitigation, then subsidies might improve efficiency by discouraging excessive mitigation. Under the opposite conditions—that is, if businesses that underestimate the risk consider insurance a good substitute for mitigation or businesses that overestimate the risk do not—subsidies could reduce economic efficiency and surcharges might be appropriate.

Other arguments hold that even if insurers and businesses have reasonably accurate perceptions of terrorism risk, the resulting market price of terrorism insurance would nonetheless be too high from society's point of view, and thus would justify some degree of federal subsidies. CBO has identified three such arguments.

- Because acts of terrorism are directed at the country as a whole, not specifically at the owners and users of particular facilities targeted for their patriotic or iconic value, federal subsidies that distribute some of the cost of terrorism risk to taxpayers as a whole may be seen as fair.

- Insurance coverage may have spillover benefits not taken into account by potential policyholders. For example, widespread coverage may help to maintain general economic stability after a large attack. Spillover benefits may also arise from concentrations of certain types of economic activity in specific parts of urban areas. An example of such "agglomeration effects" is rapid diffusion of knowledge and information among a dense grouping of related businesses in a large city's central business district. Federal subsidies that reflect the extent of such spillover benefits could improve economic efficiency.

- Subsidies that encourage more businesses to purchase terrorism insurance reduce government costs after an attack by lowering tax deductions for uninsured losses and perhaps by reducing demands for disaster assistance (though again, relatively little of such assistance goes to businesses). On their own, those reductions in government costs probably do not justify subsidies—that is, subsidies are unlikely to "pay for themselves": Because demand for terrorism insurance is relatively insensitive to price, any subsidies primarily benefit policyholders who would have purchased coverage anyway, thus yielding no reductions in tax deductions or demands for aid. [17]

Arguments Against Federal Involvement. Most arguments against an explicit federal insurance program for terrorism risk focus on the negative effects of subsidies.[18] Subsidies are not inherent in

---

[17] Erwann Michel-Kerjan, Paul Raschky, and Howard Kunreuther, *Corporate Demand for Insurance: An Empirical Analysis of the U.S. Market for Catastrophe and Non-Catastrophe Risks*, Working Paper 17403 (National Bureau of Economic Research, September 2011), www.nber.org/papers/w17403. For an alternative view on possible savings from reductions in federal assistance after an attack, see Tom LaTourrette and Noreen Clancy, *The Impact on Federal Spending of Allowing the Terrorism Risk Insurance Act to Expire* (policy brief, RAND, April 2014), www.rand.org/pubs/research_reports/RR611.html.

[18] Other aspects of current federal involvement in terrorism insurance are less controversial because they impinge less on the markets for property and casualty insurance (as regulated by the states). For example, although TRIA requires insurers who sell commercial property and casualty policies to offer terrorism coverage in conjunction with those policies (as was already required by New York State and California), it does not restrict the premiums that insurers charge for that coverage.

federal insurance—policymakers could choose to eliminate or minimize them—but they are common in such programs.

One adverse effect of subsidized federal reinsurance is that it may increase expected losses from future terrorist attacks by reducing policyholders' efforts to mitigate the risks of their current activities. In general, the efficient response to risk involves mitigating some of it and spreading the rest through insurance. In the case of terrorism risk, private mitigation can take several forms, including relocating operations away from perceived high-risk areas; constructing new offices, plants, or other commercial buildings that are inherently more secure and enhancing the structural security of existing buildings; and putting in nonstructural improvements, such as screening and monitoring devices and biological and chemical filters in air supply systems. However, insured property owners have less incentive to invest in mitigation unless they receive discounts in their insurance premiums for doing so, and insurers receiving federal subsidies have less incentive to charge full risk-based prices and to offer appropriate mitigation discounts.

The size of any effect TRIA's subsidies are having on future losses from terrorism depends on two factors, both of which are unknown: the effectiveness of investments to mitigate terrorism risk and the extent to which the subsidies are affecting decisions on those investments. Although mitigation for natural disasters has been shown to reduce losses cost-effectively, whether private investments in mitigation of terrorist risk have comparable benefits is unclear, in part because changes in terrorists' tactics and the government's counterterrorism policies can reduce the value of a particular investment.[19]

Federal involvement in terrorism insurance probably has its greatest effects on mitigation by leading insurers to "flatten" their rates geographically, holding down the premiums they would otherwise charge in higher-risk areas (particularly the central business districts of major cities) and thus reducing policyholders' incentives to locate or relocate away from those areas. Whether the effects of federal terrorism reinsurance on other forms of mitigation are significant in practice is unclear, for four reasons. First, policyholders carrying subsidized terrorism coverage will take some mitigation measures nonetheless, as illustrated by the enhanced safety features included by the developers of the new Freedom Tower at One World Trade Center.[20] Second, subsidized premiums may have less influence on some policyholders' decisions than their expectations of receiving federal disaster assistance in the event of an attack. Third, the significant risks primary insurers retain in the form of deductibles and copayments encourage them to set premiums that take at least some account of the risks of particular policyholders— as they do by setting rates that vary across industries and by region. Fourth, insurers' use of discounted premiums for mitigation activities might be limited not only by the disincentive effect of subsidized federal reinsurance, but also by the difficulty of estimating the effects of those activities on policyholders' expected losses.

A second adverse effect of subsidized federal reinsurance is that it limits private-sector alternatives—both traditional reinsurance and newer capital market alternatives—even if it supports supply in the primary market. Private reinsurers cannot compete with subsidized federal reinsurance and are left offering

---

[19] On the effectiveness of natural disaster mitigation, see Congressional Budget Office, *Potential Cost Savings From the Pre-Disaster Mitigation Program* (September 2007), www.cbo.gov/publication/19166. An example of insurance pricing designed to encourage mitigation is the Community Rating System of the National Flood Insurance Program, which offers discounts of up to 45 percent on coverage of properties in communities that undertake various activities to reduce flood losses; see Federal Emergency Management Agency, "Community Rating System Fact Sheet" (November 2012), www.fema.gov/media-library/assets/documents/9998.

[20] See Port Authority of New York and New Jersey, "One World Trade Center," www.panynj.gov/wtcprogress/index.html; and Skidmore, Owings, and Merrill, "World Trade Center Tower One Freedom Tower" (architectural fact sheet, June 2005), http://renewnyc.com/content/pdfs/freedom_tower_fact_sheet.pdf.

coverage only for the risks retained by the primary insurers.[21] Participation by private reinsurers allows risks to be shared globally and encourages innovations in coverage that could further improve that risk distribution in the future. Reinsurers also frequently have more expertise than primary insurers in valuing catastrophic risk.

A third argument against federal subsidies, particularly those that reduce the cost of insurance in higher-risk areas, is that a decision by one business to locate in such an area may have costs for the other businesses there, if concentrating attractive targets increases the overall likelihood of a terrorist attack. That argument is the mirror image of the argument that agglomeration effects may justify subsidies for certain policyholders in certain areas; it suggests that some insurance policies should carry surcharges on top of the premiums based on expected losses.

The Federal Terrorism Risk Insurance Program

In response to the problems observed in insurance markets after the September 11 attacks, lawmakers passed the Terrorism Risk Insurance Act in November 2002. As stated in the original statute, TRIA was intended as a temporary measure to help insurers recover from the losses they incurred and to give the industry time to develop more accurate ways of pricing terrorism risk. Lawmakers have extended the program three times, and in doing so have shifted some costs and risks away from the government and toward insurers, who are in a better financial position to bear them now than they were in 2002.[22] The most recent extension, The Terrorism Risk Insurance Program Reauthorization Act of 2015 (P.L. 114-1), enacted in January 2015, continues the program through 2020.

Under TRIA, all commercial property and casualty insurers (who cover losses to businesses from damage or injuries that occur on an insured property) must offer their policyholders terrorism coverage. The federal government backstops that coverage by providing "catastrophic reinsurance" against losses from terrorist attacks. If a sufficiently large attack occurs, insurers pay an initial layer of losses up to their individual deductibles and then a fraction of the losses over that amount, and the federal government pays the rest.[23] The program caps liability for insurers and the government at $100 billion per year; policyholders are not compensated for terrorism losses above that cap. Unlike private reinsurers, the government does not charge up-front premiums but instead recoups (recovers) at least some of its spending on claims by taxing all commercial policyholders after an attack.

Because of the required recoupments, the expected net budgetary costs from the program are very low. However, unlikely attacks comparable to or bigger than the attacks on the World Trade Center could result in significant federal outlays that may not be completely recouped.

TRIA has had several effects on insurance markets. For example, by reducing the price of terrorism coverage—insurers do not have to pay reinsurance premiums for TRIA coverage, and competition ensures that the resulting cost savings flow to policyholders—the program has helped to increase the

---

[21] To avoid or reduce subsidies and encourage more reinsurance capacity, Australia's government-backed terrorism insurance pool buys private reinsurance; for details, see the appendix.

[22] For more analysis of the program, see Government Accountability Office, *Terrorism Insurance*, GAO-14-445 (June 2014), www.gao.gov/products/GAO-14-445; and Baird Webel, *Terrorism Risk Insurance: Issue Analysis and Overview of Current Program*, Report for Congress R42716 (Congressional Research Service, July 23, 2014). The current statutory language is available at www.treasury.gov/resource-center/fin-mkts/Documents/TRIAasamended-CompositeTextPost.pdf.

[23] TRIA does not affect the regulation of insurers, which continues to be handled primarily at the state level; federal oversight is limited except in the case of insurers that have been designated as systemically important financial institutions.

percentage of policyholders that include terrorism coverage in their policies. On the downside, it has limited the opportunities for private reinsurers to offer terrorism coverage.

Although TRIA may have helped speed recovery in the New York City area after the September 11 attacks, its effects on the economy as a whole have probably been small. The program could have larger benefits after a future attack by minimizing any disruption of insurance coverage; but it could have costs as well, if losses from an attack were larger because policyholders undertook less mitigation than they would have in the absence of the program's implicit insurance subsidies.

How TRIA Works

Through its reinsurance under TRIA, the federal government covers insured losses from property damage, workers' compensation, business interruption, and many types of liability claims. Losses on other types of insurance (including home, health, and life) are not covered; the markets for those types of insurance were not significantly disrupted after the September 11 attacks.

TRIA does not require that insurers provide coverage for losses from nuclear, biological, chemical, or radiological risks, which typically were excluded by insurers before 9/11 and continue to be excluded from most policies today. The major exception is for workers' compensation insurance; state regulations allow virtually no exclusions for that type of coverage. The federal program reinsures NBCR coverage when it is included in a policy. Many policies also exclude cyber risks, but when they are included, they are covered by TRIA.[24]

Under the "make available" requirement, terrorism insurance cannot differ materially from the terms, amounts, and limitations that apply to coverage for losses from nonterrorist events. There are no restrictions on pricing, but the charge for terrorism risk coverage has to be disclosed separately to the policyholder. The program does not cover reinsurers.

Under TRIA, private insurers, policyholders, and the government share terrorism risks. The responsibility for losses from a particular attack certified as a terrorist act by the Secretary of the Treasury depends on several factors. Those factors, as modified by the 2015 reauthorization, are as follows:[25]

- The amount of losses triggering payments under the program increases by $20 million per year from a base of $100 million in 2015 to $200 million in 2020.

- Each insurer with losses from an attack has a deductible, currently defined as 20 percent of its prior-year premiums for all insurance lines covered by TRIA. (Only a small share of those premiums is for terrorism coverage itself.)

- TRIA caps the total combined liability of private insurers and the government at $100 billion per year. If one or more attacks in a year cause insured losses greater than $100 billion, policyholders are not compensated for losses above that amount. (Claims for insured losses exceeding $100 billion are to be prorated, though the process for doing so is not specified in the law.)

---

[24] Robert Hartwig and Claire Wilkinson, *Cyber Risks: The Growing Threat* (Insurance Information Institute, June 2014), www.iii.org/white-paper/cyber-risks-the-growing-threat-062714.

[25] H.R. 26 is identical to S. 2244, which passed the House of Representatives on December 10, 2014, in the 113th Congress. See Congressional Budget Office, *Federal Reinsurance for Terrorism Risk: An Update* (January 2015), pp. 5–7, www.cbo.gov/publication/49866.

- For losses below the $100 billion cap, each insurer pays a portion of its losses above its deductible—15 percent in 2015, rising by 1 percentage point per year to 20 percent in 2020—and the government pays the rest.

- The private sector retains responsibility for losses up to an "aggregate retention amount." That amount is $29.5 billion in 2015 and increases by $2 billion per year to $37.5 billion in 2019; in 2020, the retention amount equals the average of insurers' deductibles over the previous three years (about $50 billion, CBO estimated). If insurers' deductibles and copayments do not cover all losses below the retention amount, the government recoups the rest by taxing all commercial property and casualty policyholders after an attack—even those who chose not to purchase terrorism coverage.[26] Under the current reauthorization, the tax rate is set to yield 140 percent of the federal outlays to be recouped.[27]

- For attacks that cause losses greater than the retention amount, the Secretary of the Treasury has the discretion to extend recoupment to recover some or all of the outlays corresponding to the losses above that amount.

If the recoupment mechanism works as intended, the aggregate retention amount will be high enough that insurers and commercial policyholders would bear all or almost all of the losses that would follow an attack similar in size to the 9/11 attacks, while the government's losses would be small or zero. However, because no such attack has occurred under TRIA, the imposition of taxes—potentially totaling billions of dollars—on commercial policyholders, including those with no insured losses and even those without terrorism coverage, has not yet been tested.

The effects of TRIA's various risk-sharing provisions as they apply in 2015 are illustrated in Figure 1. The two panels of the figure show the allocations of losses under two scenarios involving different groups of insurers and different proportional distributions of losses among those insurers. Either panel in Figure 1 can be used to identify the allocation of losses for any size of attack for which its specified scenario about the affected insurers and the distribution of the losses applies. In general, however, scenarios like the one shown in Panel A, involving smaller groups of insurers, would be more likely to apply to smaller attacks. Conversely, larger attacks would probably involve larger groups of insurers, such as the group represented in Panel B.

---

[26] Lawmakers have required assessments after an attack in other circumstances, when establishing accurate premiums up front is challenging. For example, the Orderly Liquidation Fund established by the Dodd-Frank Wall Street Reform and Consumer Protection Act of 2010 relies on such assessments on banks to recover the budgetary costs of resolving failures of systemically important financial institutions. In addition, under the Price-Anderson Nuclear Industries Indemnity Act of 1957, nuclear reactor operators could face assessments to recoup some of the losses in the event of a nuclear accident; see National Association of Insurance Commissioners and the Center for Insurance Policy Research, "Nuclear Liability Insurance (Price-Anderson Act)" (November 11, 2014), www.naic.org/cipr_topics/topic_nuclear_liability_insurance.htm. However, the largest losses to date—from the Three-Mile Island nuclear accident—were covered by primary insurers. No assessments under those two laws have been collected. Assessments on property and casualty insurers have been used by many state guaranty funds, which cover some of the claims of insolvent insurers. See Insurance Information Institute, *Insolvencies/Guaranty Funds* (issue update, September 2014); www.iii.org/issue-update/insolvencies-guaranty-funds.

[27] Previously, the tax rate was to be set so as to yield 133 percent of the outlays to be recouped. The additional 33 percent helped make the 2007 amendments to TRIA roughly budget neutral because it compensated for the corporate tax receipts that would be lost as policyholders deducted the recoupment charges from their taxable income. Under Congressional scoring rules, the budget estimates for the 2007 amendments reduced the net revenue from the recoupments by 25 percent to account for the lower income and payroll tax receipts; the additional 33 percent recoupment offset that reduction because $(1 - 0.25)*1.33$ approximately equals 1. Setting the tax to yield 140 percent of the outlays being recouped provides some additional compensation to the government for bearing risk.

Figure 1.
Allocation of Potential 2015 Losses Under Two Exposure Scenarios

(Allocation of losses, billions of dollars)

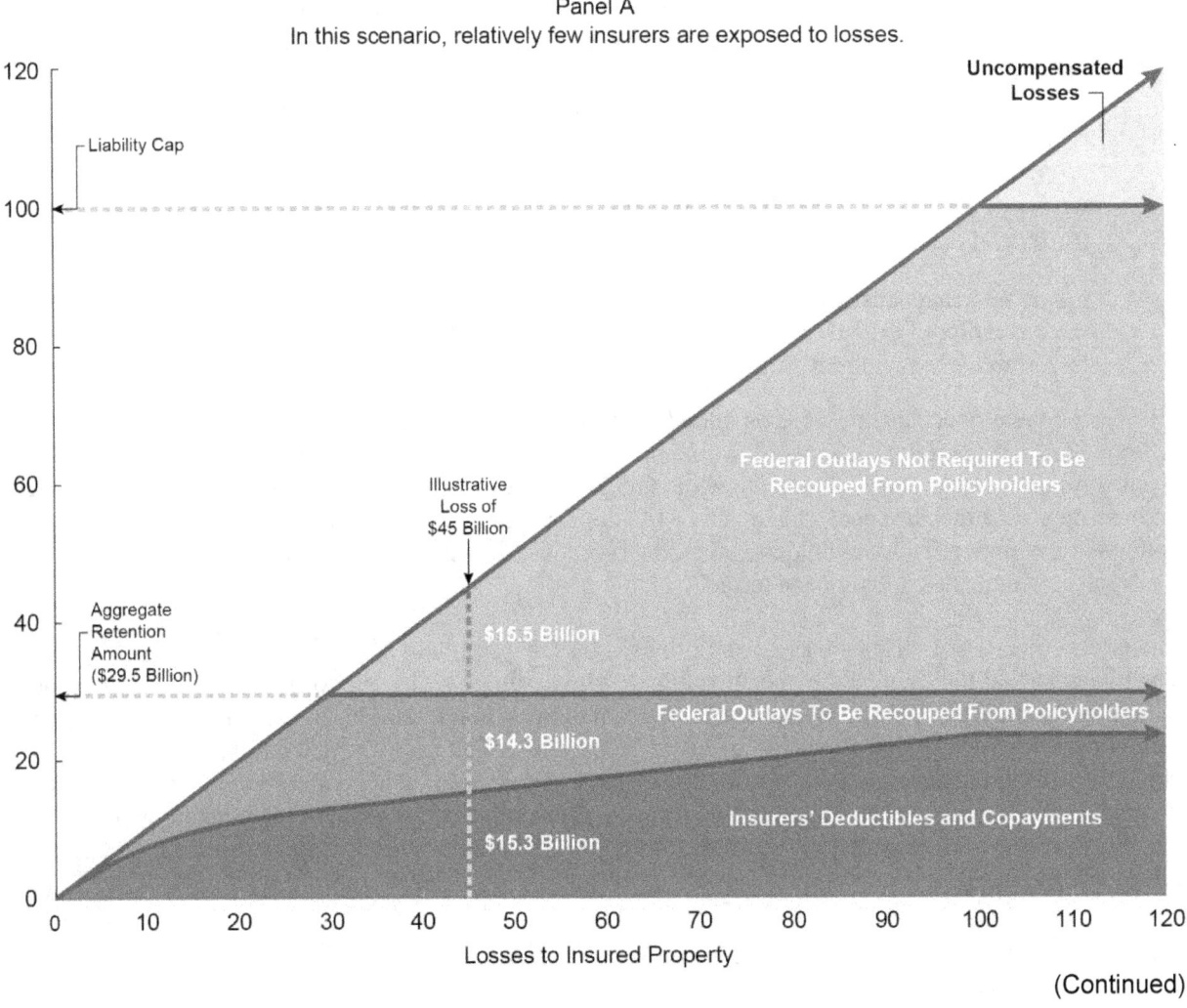

Panel A
In this scenario, relatively few insurers are exposed to losses.

For the scenario depicted in Panel A, the losses would be spread rather unevenly among a group of insurers that have collective deductibles of $10 billion (about one-fourth of the roughly $40 billion aggregate deductible for all insurers). Specifically, given the distribution pattern of the losses among the insurers, only attacks that caused losses of $30 billion or more would result in all insurers reaching their deductibles.[28] To illustrate the scenario, a hypothetical attack that caused $45 billion in insured losses (making it roughly as costly as the September 11 attacks) is shown as a dashed line in Figure 1. With such

---

[28] An equivalent way to specify the scenario is to say that 1:3 is the lowest ratio of an affected insurer's share of losses to its market share (which determines its share of the collective $10 billion deductible). For example, one insurer might have 1.2 percent of the group's total market share, corresponding to an individual deductible of $0.12 billion, but only 0.4 percent of the losses. Such an insurer would meet its deductible on a collective loss of $30 billion or more, because 0.4 percent of $30 billion is $0.12 billion. For simplicity, the scenario also reflects the assumption that the group of affected insurers comprises a large number of small firms, implying a smooth trajectory of insurers' contributions as the amount of insured losses increases from

Figure 1. (Continued)
Allocation of Potential 2015 Losses Under Two Exposure Scenarios

(Allocation of losses, billions of dollars)

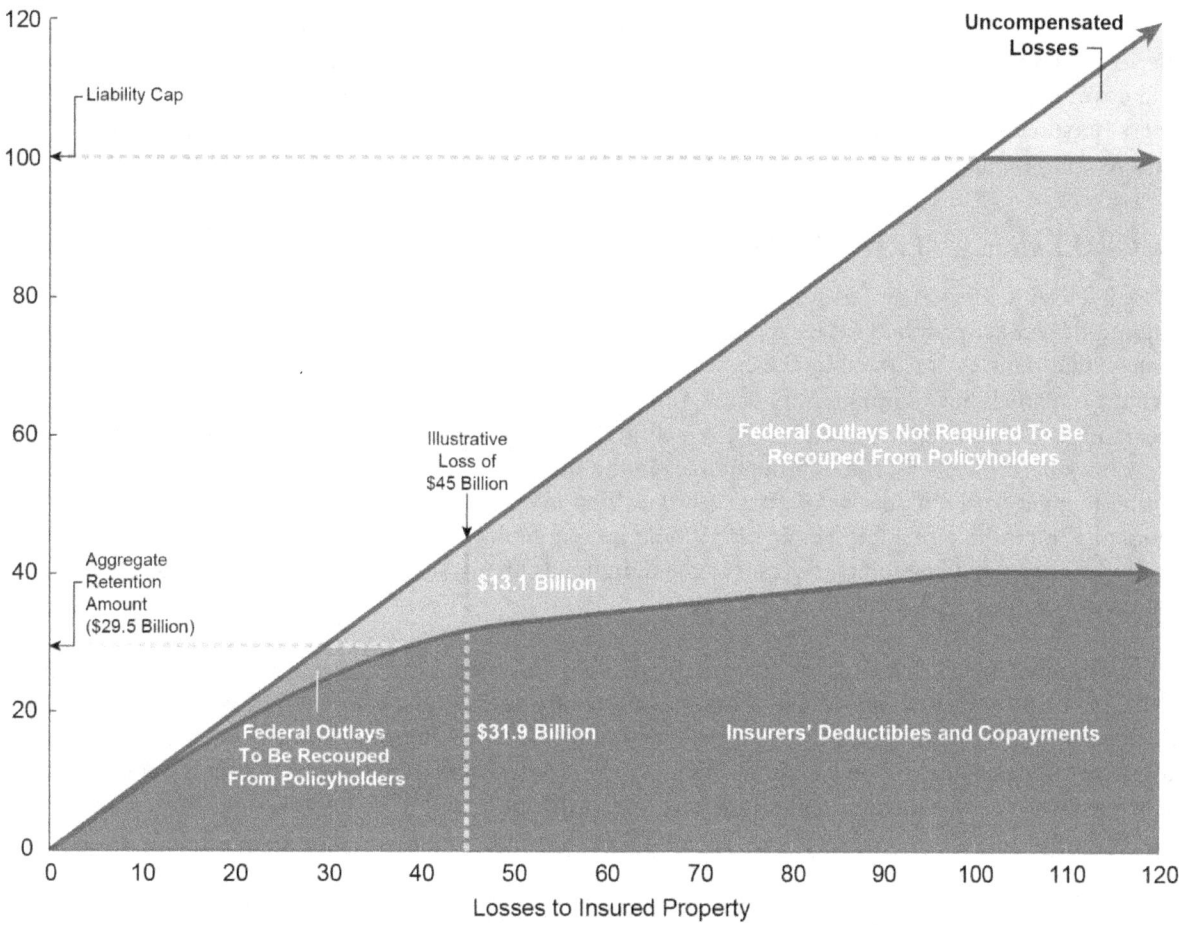

Panel B
In this scenario, losses are spread more widely among insurers.

Source: Congressional Budget Office.

Note: For a particular attack, the losses paid by insurers in deductibles and copayments depend on the total insured losses, the total deductibles of the affected insurers, and the proportional distribution of the losses among those insurers. Panel A shows the allocations of losses for attacks of different sizes that affect an illustrative set of insurers with collective deductibles of $10 billion and that distribute the losses among them such that all of the insurers meet their deductibles if total insured losses are $30 billion or more; Panel B shows the allocations for attacks of different sizes that affect insurers with collective deductibles of $30 billion and that distribute the losses among them such that all meet their deductibles if insured losses are $50 billion or more. Both panels reflect the 15 percent copayment rate and the $29.5 billion aggregate retention amount in effect in 2015. (They also reflect an assumption that each individual insurer is small and thus that the curves representing total insurers' deductibles and copayments are smooth. Because of that smoothness the curves in the two panels appear to flatten out, reaching slopes of about 15 percent, for losses of less than $30 billion and $50 billion, respectively; however, they remain very slightly curved below those thresholds.)

---

zero to $30 billion and more insurers switch from paying deductibles to 15 percent copayments. Assuming a rougher trajectory would not significantly affect CBO's analysis.

an attack, $15.25 billion of the insured losses would be covered by insurers' deductibles and copayments; of the remaining $29.75 billion covered by federal outlays, the Treasury would be required to recoup $14.25 billion but not required to recoup $15.5 billion.[29]

In contrast, Panel B in Figure 1 shows loss allocations under a scenario in which losses were spread among insurers with total deductibles of $30 billion and were distributed somewhat more proportionately, so that the $30 billion would be reached if total insured losses were $50 billion or more.[30] Under that scenario, for an attack that caused $45 billion in insured losses, insurers' deductibles and copayments would cover almost $32 billion and federal outlays would cover the remaining $13 billion. Because the insurers' payments would exceed the aggregate retention amount of $29.5 billion, the Treasury would not be required to recoup any of the federal outlays.

How CBO Estimates TRIA's Budgetary Costs

Although TRIA has led to no federal outlays or revenues since its inception (because no attacks big enough to trigger the program have occurred), the program does affect projections of federal spending and revenues; that point is illustrated by the expected budgetary cost for H.R. 26 (enacted as Public Law 114-1), which extended the program for six years, through calendar year 2020. [31] CBO estimated that, over the 10 years from 2015 to 2025, extending TRIA would increase federal spending by $3.1 billion and boost net revenues by about $3.5 billion through taxes in the form of surcharges imposed on policyholders, resulting in a net deficit reduction of about $400 million over the period. Taking into account an additional $260 million that CBO estimated would be spent after 2025 (because some claims would not be settled before then), the total reduction in the deficit was about $120 million (leaving aside any potential effect on spending for disaster relief).

Effect on Spending. CBO estimated that reauthorizing TRIA would increase direct spending by about $3.4 billion on an expected-value basis—that is, taking into account the estimated probabilities of losses of all sizes—of which $3.1 billion would occur within the 2015–2025 projection period. That amount reflected estimates made by some commercial catastrophe modelers that expected losses from terrorist attacks have fallen since the program's previous reauthorization in 2007.[32] CBO estimated that expected losses from attacks that would be covered under TRIA, most of which would be covered by insurers'

---

[29] The $15.25 billion paid by insurers includes their collective deductibles of $10 billion (which are all met because the total insured loss exceeds $30 billion) and copayments of $5.25 billion (the 15 percent copayment rate times the $35 billion of losses above the deductibles).

[30] An equivalent description of the distribution is that the lowest ratio of an affected insurer's share of losses to its market share is 3:5. For example, an insurer might have 1.5 percent of the group's market share, corresponding to an individual deductible of $0.45 billion, but 0.9 percent of the losses. That insurer would meet its deductible on a collective loss of $50 billion.

[31] The bill also contained other provisions that are unrelated to terrorism insurance. See Congressional Budget Office, cost estimate for H.R. 26, Terrorism Risk Insurance Program Reauthorization Act of 2015 (January 8, 2015), www.cbo.gov/publication/49888. In addition, see the cost estimate for the version of the bill reported by the House Committee on Financial Services [Congressional Budget Office, cost estimate for H.R. 4871, the TRIA Reform Act of 2014 (July 15, 2014), www.cbo.gov/publication/45535] and the cost estimate for the version reported by the Senate Committee on Banking, Housing, and Urban Affairs [Congressional Budget Office, cost estimate for S. 2244, the Terrorism Risk Insurance Program Reauthorization Act of 2014 (June 24, 2014), www.cbo.gov/publication/45474]. Also see Baird Webel, *Terrorism Risk Insurance Legislation: Issue Summary and Side-by-Side Analysis*, CRS Report for Congress R43619 (Congressional Research Service, December 11, 2014). Consistent with Congressional budget-scoring principles, the estimate did not consider the potential effects of TRIA on the costs of future Congressional action, such as action to provide disaster assistance or to reduce taxes after a future terrorist attack.

[32] For a discussion of changes made by terrorism modelers, see Guy Carpenter & Company, *Uncertain Future: Evolving Terrorism Risk* (June 2014), pp. 22–25, http://tinyurl.com/p5oawt9.

deductibles and copayments, would be about $2.1 billion in 2015, rising each year with projected growth in the economy. Those average amounts incorporated a wide and unevenly distributed set of possibilities, ranging from no attacks in a year to highly unlikely catastrophic attacks.

Effect on Revenues. CBO's estimate of net revenues, $3.5 billion over the 2015-2025 period, reflected the law's requirement that all amounts due under the program's recoupment provisions be collected by September 30, 2024. The law requires the Secretary of the Treasury to recoup federal payments to the extent that the total amount paid by insurers (for deductibles and the industry's share of payments over the deductibles) is less than the lower of total insured losses or the aggregate retention amount. Thus, the government would ultimately recoup all federal payments for insured losses that are less than the retention amount ($29.5 billion in 2015).

Furthermore, the recoupment provisions require that the Secretary collect 140 percent of the difference between the retention amount and the amount paid by insurers for deductibles and copayments. Net revenue collections (taking into account the effect of reduced revenues from policyholders' share of income and payroll taxes) would slightly exceed actual outlays when insured losses were less than the aggregate retention amount. CBO assumed that the Secretary would not seek to recover financial assistance provided above the retention amount and would not collect interest on outstanding amounts.

The projected receipts from the surcharges that would be imposed after an attack were critical to keeping the program roughly budget neutral. The recoupment mechanism has yet to be tested, and after a very large attack, policymakers might be hesitant to tax all commercial policyholders, including those without terrorism insurance, especially if the economy is weak.[33] If lawmakers decided to delay, reduce, or eliminate those surcharges rather than risk further weakening insurers and their policyholders after a major attack, then the program could have positive net budgetary costs over the 10-year period.

For the same reason, CBO's cost estimates for the legislation were sensitive to the specified recoupment scaling factor and pace of recoupment. For example, if policymakers had set recoupment at 100 percent of the government's outlays under the aggregate retention amount while keeping the bill's requirement that all outlays be recouped by 2024, revenues would have been lower and the program would have had an estimated net budgetary cost of about $900 million.[34] Alternatively, if policymakers had set recoupment at 140 percent, as in the bill, but allowed losses to be recouped over the 10 years following an attack rather than by 2024, the estimated net cost over the 10-year budget period would have been about $1 billion higher (because less of the expected recoupment would be received within the next 10 years); the projected net budgetary cost over all years would have been roughly the same, however.

Insurance Markets Under TRIA

TRIA has been successful in supporting the availability of terrorism coverage in commercial and property insurance policies.[35] Premiums have generally been falling, in part because no major losses have been

---

[33] Alternatively, the budgetary costs of outlays from a terrorist attack could be spread more broadly through some combination of higher general tax revenues and lower government spending.

[34] CBO's estimates are presented on a cash basis. The estimate of the net reduction in the deficit over all years would be very similar in present-value terms, because CBO expects that some outlays would occur earlier than recoupments whereas others would occur later. (Present value is a single number that expresses a flow of current and future income or payments in terms of an equivalent lump sum received or paid today.)

[35] Report of the President's Working Group on Financial Markets, *The Long-Term Availability and Affordability of Insurance for Terrorism Risk* (April 2014), www.treasury.gov/press_releases/Pages/j12365.aspx; and Erwann Michel-Kerjan and Paul Raschky,

Figure 2.
Firms Whose Property Insurance Covers Losses From Terrorism

(Percent)

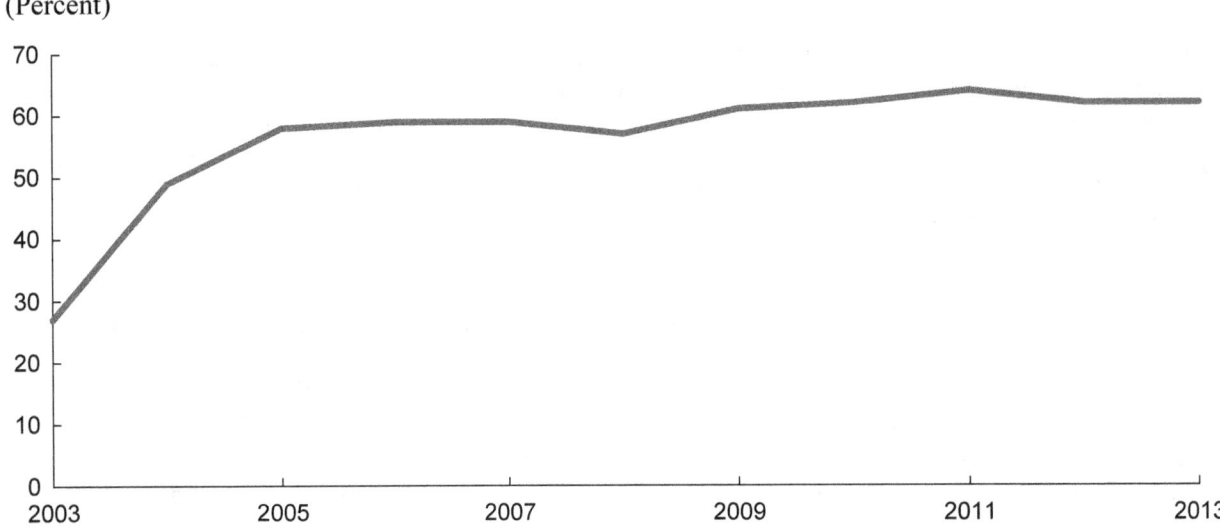

Source: Congressional Budget Office based on data from Marsh Risk Management Research.

Notes: The data from Marsh Risk Management Research came from surveys of their clients, who are mainly large- and medium-size businesses. Little is known about terrorism insurance coverage for small firms.

The data do not include coverage for workers' compensation, which is nearly 100 percent because of state regulations.

incurred, and the percentage of policyholders that purchase terrorism coverage has stabilized. The financial position of both insurers and private reinsurers is stronger than when TRIA was last reauthorized, which suggests that their ability to bear terrorism risk has increased. However, the provision of unpriced federal reinsurance limits the market for private reinsurance and for alternative methods of sharing risks in capital markets.

Primary Property and Casualty Insurance. With TRIA in place, most large and medium-size businesses purchase and maintain terrorism coverage for conventional terrorist attacks; that coverage is sold by hundreds of insurers around the country.[36] Insurance brokers, whose clients are primarily large and medium-size businesses, reported that for the past 10 years about 60 percent of their customers included such coverage in their purchases of property and casualty insurance, more than twice the percentage that bought such coverage in 2003 (see Figure 2).[37] (Much less is known about terrorism

"The Effects of Government Intervention on the Market for Corporate Terrorism Insurance," *European Journal of Political Economy*, vol. 27, supplement 1 (2011), pp. S122–S132, www.sciencedirect.com/science/article/pii/S0176268011000334.

[36]The top 30 insurers, as measured by premiums earned in TRIA-covered lines, sell about two-thirds of total terrorism coverage. See Howard Kunreuther and others, *TRIA After 2014: Examining Risk Sharing Under Current and Alternative Designs* (The Wharton School, University of Pennsylvania, Summer 2014, p. 19); http://opim.wharton.upenn.edu/risk/library/TRIA-after-2014_full-report_WhartonRiskCenter.pdf (1,691 KB).

[37] Marsh Risk Management Research, *Terrorism Risk Insurance Report* (April 2014), http://usa.marsh.com/NewsInsights/MarshRiskManagementResearch/ID/2781/2014-Terrorism-Risk-Insurance-Report.aspx. Aon, another broker, reports somewhat higher coverage rates but the same pattern; see Aon, *Response to U.S. Treasury and President's Working Group: Terrorism (Re)insurance* (September 2013), www.regulations.gov/#!documentDetail;D=TREAS-DO-2013-0003-0028.

Figure 3.
Median Rates per $1 Million of Coverage for Terrorism Insurance, by Insured Value, 2003 to 2013

(Dollars)

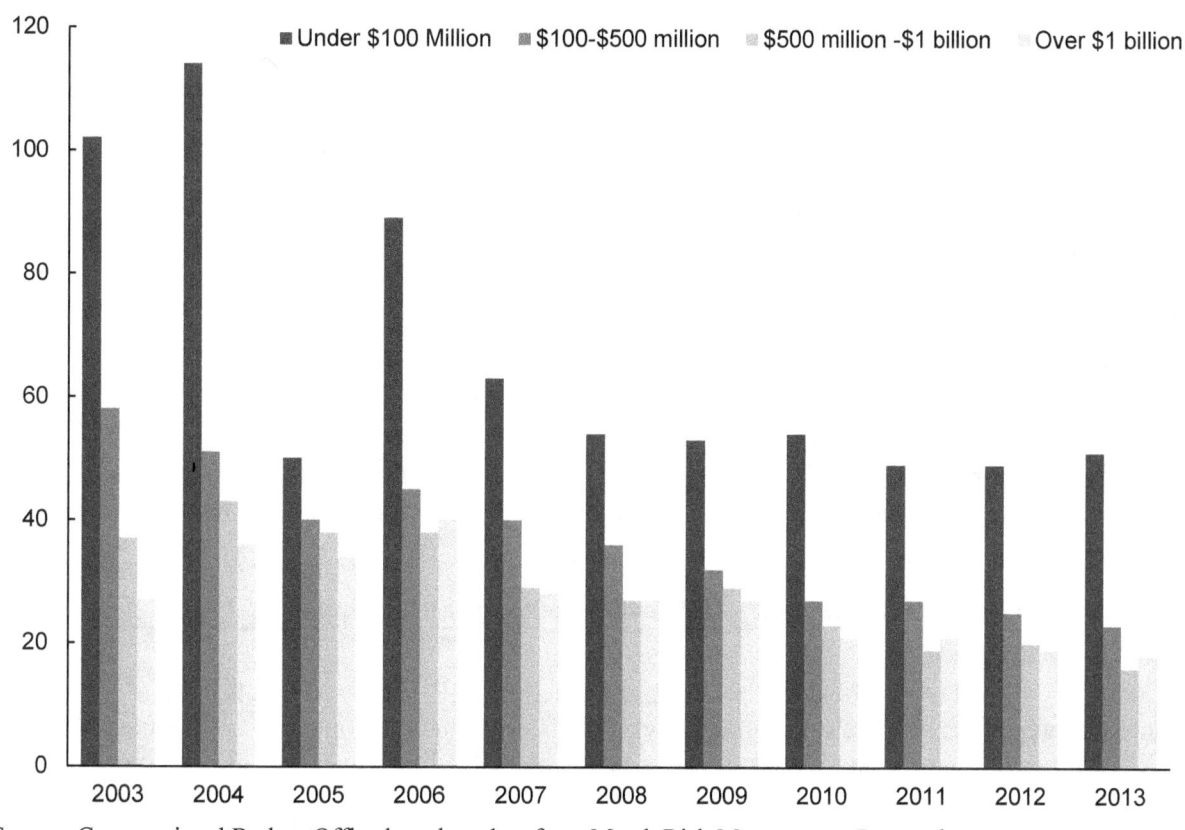

Source: Congressional Budget Office based on data from Marsh Risk Management Research.

coverage for small businesses.) Take-up rates vary by industry and region; coverage is greatest in the Northeast, where the terrorist threat is presumed to be highest.[38]

In contrast, coverage for NBCR terrorist attacks (except for workers' compensation policies, discussed below) is not widely purchased.[39] Few insurers offer NBCR coverage, and limits are low and premiums per dollar of coverage are high, compared with the terms of coverage for conventional terrorist attacks.[40]

---

[38] Requirements imposed by lenders can motivate firms and property owners to buy coverage: Terrorism insurance covered about $1 trillion of the $1.5 trillion of loan balances for commercial and multifamily mortgages surveyed in 2013. See Mortgage Bankers Association, "MBA 2013 Survey of Terrorism Insurance Coverage" (May 5, 2014).

[39] Report of the President's Working Group on Financial Markets, *Market Conditions for Terrorism Risk Insurance 2010* (January 2011), www.treasury.gov/resource-center/fin-mkts/Pages/resources.aspx; and Government Accountability Office, *Terrorism Insurance: Status of Efforts by Policyholders to Obtain Coverage*, GAO-09-1057 (September 2008), www.gao.gov/products/GAO-08-1057.

[40] Aon, *Response to U.S. Treasury and President's Working Group: Terrorism (Re)insurance* (September 2013), pp. 26–27, www.regulations.gov/#!documentDetail;D=TREAS-DO-2013-0003-0028.

Figure 4.
Estimated Premiums for Private Terrorism Insurance, 2004 to 2013

(Millions of 2014 dollars)

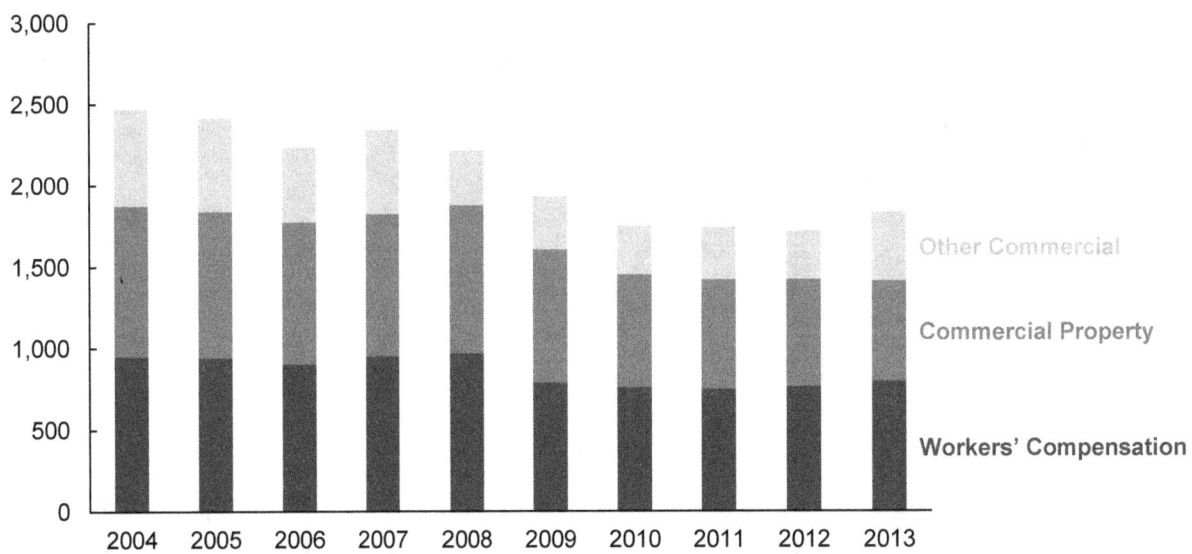

Source: Congressional Budget Office based on data from A.M. Best.

Note: "Other Commercial" coverage includes business interruption and liability policies.

Prices paid by policyholders for terrorism coverage have declined steadily even as changes to TRIA have required insurers to retain more risks through higher deductibles and copayments. For example, the median price fell by more than 50 percent between 2003 and 2013 for businesses with total insured values between $500 million and $1 billion (see Figure 3). According to one estimate, between 2004 and 2013 premiums paid by policyholders for terrorism coverage fell from about $2.5 billion to less than $2 billion (in 2014 dollars); see Figure 4.[41] Current rates are typically between 3 percent and 6 percent of the total property premiums.[42] However, the falling prices have had relatively little effect on insurance coverage: Corporate demand for terrorism coverage appears to be largely insensitive to price.[43]

The workers' compensation market accounts for about 40 percent of terrorism insurance premiums. TRIA made it easier for insurers to continue to offer coverage and also relieved pressure on the involuntary segment of the market—a "residual market" established by many states for businesses that cannot obtain

---

[41] One credit-rating agency has somewhat higher estimates. Standard & Poor's estimates that about $25 billion in premiums has been collected for commercial property terrorism coverage. See Tracy Dolin and others, "TRIPRA on the Brink of Expiration: A Ratings Perspective," *RatingsDirect* (Standard & Poor's, March 17, 2014), p. 4.

[42] Prices tend to be lowest in the Midwest and South and highest in the Northeast. See Marsh Risk Management Research, *2014 Terrorism Risk Insurance Report* (April 2014), p. 19.

[43] Studies have found that a 10 percent decrease in price would increase terrorism coverage by between 1 percent and 2.5 percent compared with an increase of 2 percent to 3.5 percent for general property coverage. See Erwann Michel-Kerjan, Paul Raschky, and Howard Kunreuther, *Do Firms Manage Catastrophe and Non-Catastrophe Risk Differently?* Working Paper 2011-13 (Wharton Risk Management and Decision Processes Center, December 4, 2011), http://opim.wharton.upenn.edu/risk/library/ WP2011-13_EMK-PAR-HCK.pdf (642 KB) ; and Erwann Michel-Kerjan, Paul Raschky, and Howard Kunreuther, *Corporate Demand for Insurance: An Empirical Analysis of the U.S. Market for Catastrophe and Non-Catastrophe Risks*, Working Paper 17403 (National Bureau of Economic Research, September 2011), www.nber.org/papers/w17403.

coverage in the voluntary market.[44] Workers' compensation is heavily regulated at the state level. According to the National Council on Compensation Insurance, most states set terrorism loss costs—the portion of the premium that covers expected losses but not the insurers' administrative costs or targeted return on capital—at $0.01 per $100 of payroll in 2013, down from an average of roughly $0.02 per $100 in 2006, although allowed costs are higher in some jurisdictions.[45] Those regulations affect the willingness of insurers to supply coverage and make the market potentially vulnerable to disruption after an attack in the absence of a federal backstop.[46]

Private Reinsurance. Reinsurance helps primary insurers manage their catastrophic risks, particularly those that are concentrated in specific areas, and thus allows them to take on more risk.[47] Private reinsurers cannot compete against free federal reinsurance, but they do sell reinsurance to cover some of the risks retained by the primary insurers under TRIA. Insurers may purchase reinsurance that covers many types of risk for some of their insured properties or that covers only terrorism risk for individual properties. Prices for that reinsurance have been falling.[48] Domestic insurers purchase an estimated $7 billion to $8 billion of coverage each year specifically for conventional terrorism risk (excluding reinsurance for general property and casualty coverage and workers' compensation coverage) from private reinsurers around the world, and some industry participants believe that reinsurers have additional capacity not yet tapped for conventional terrorism risks.[49] For NBCR risks, almost no coverage was available for many years, other than small amounts for workers' compensation policies, and reinsurers' willingness to take on more NBCR risk still remains very limited.[50]

Terrorism risk could also be spread in the capital markets through insurance-linked securities, which pay off if a specified insurance loss occurs. Capital markets play a small but growing role in bearing risks from natural disasters but a very minor role in backing terrorism risk.[51]

---

[44] National Council on Compensation Insurance, "Re: President's Working Group on Financial Markets: Terrorism Risk Insurance Analysis" (September 16, 2013), www.regulations.gov/#!documentDetail;D=TREAS-DO-2013-0003-0026. Insurers voluntarily writing coverage generally bear a share of the costs of operating the states' residual plans.

[45] For example, insurers may charge $0.05 per $100 of payroll in the District of Columbia and $0.038 per $100 in New York State.

[46] For additional details, see Congressional Budget Office, *Federal Reinsurance for Terrorism Risks: Issues in Reauthorization* (August 2007), pp. 8–9; www.cbo.gov/publication/19035.

[47] Andy Polacek, "How Do Property and Casualty Insurers Manage Risk? The Role of Reinsurance," *Chicago Fed Letter*, no. 334 (2015), www.chicagofed.org/publications/chicago-fed-letter/2015/334.

[48] Guy Carpenter Co., *Uncertain Future: Evolving Terrorism Risk* (June 2014), pp. 17–18, www.guycarp.com/content/dam/guycarp/en/documents/dynamic-content/Uncertain%20Future_Evolving%20Terrorism%20Risk_June%202014.pdf (2,155 KB).

[49] For example, see testimony of Kean Driscoll, chief executive officer, Validus Re, before the Subcommittee on Housing and Insurance of the House Committee on Financial Services (November 13, 2013), http://financialservices.house.gov/uploadedfiles/hhrg-113-ba04-wstate-kdriscoll-20131113.pdf (303KB).

[50] Marsh and McLennan Cos., "Re: Request for Comments on the President's Working Group on Financial Markets: The Long-Term Availability and Affordability of Insurance for Terrorism Risk" (September 16, 2013), www.regulations.gov/#!documentDetail;D=TREAS-DO-2013-0003-0027.

[51] See Congressional Budget Office, *Federal Reinsurance for Terrorism Risks: Issues in Reauthorization* (August 2007), pp. 29–31, www.cbo.gov/publication/19035; and testimony of John S. Seo, cofounder and managing principal, Fermat Capital Management, before the Subcommittee on Housing and Insurance of the House Committee on Financial Services (November 13, 2013), http://financialservices.house.gov/calendar/eventsingle.aspx?EventID=360497. The Australian Reinsurance Pool Corporation (see the appendix) considered purchasing indexed-linked securities for its terrorism risk program but found the price too high relative to that of traditional private reinsurance. Personal communication to the Congressional Budget Office from Michael Pennell, Australian Reinsurance Pool Corporation, March 18, 2015.

Financial Position of Insurers. Insurers' capital, or the excess of assets over liabilities, indicates the resources available to them to offset unexpected losses before facing bankruptcy and is thus a key measure of their financial position.[52] To meet state requirements for minimum capital ratios and protect their credit rating, insurers manage their exposure to terrorism risk by limiting the policies they write to a fraction of their capital. They can raise additional capital—for example, by issuing stock or retaining more of their earnings—but doing so takes time, especially after large losses have been incurred.

Property and casualty insurers' reported capital has increased significantly in recent years—from about $290 billion in 2002 to $520 billion at the end of 2007 and more than $670 billion in June 2014.[53] Not all of the additional capital is available to pay terrorism claims. But the growth suggests that insurers would probably be able to raise additional capital if they had to take on more terrorism risk.

Private reinsurers' reported capital backing property and casualty risks has also grown in recent years, from about $200 billion worldwide in 2007 to more than $300 billion in 2013.[54] With capital available and somewhat increased confidence in their ability to model and price risks from attacks using conventional weapons, reinsurers are willing to bear more conventional terrorism risk. (And if profitable opportunities to insure terrorism risk exceeded reinsurers' supplies of capital, they could raise additional capital, as they have done to increase their coverage of natural disasters.) By some estimates, reinsurers could cover most of the current aggregate retention amount under TRIA ($27.5 billion) under current market conditions either by raising new capital or by reallocating their existing capital.[55] There is probably a limit to the capital that investors would be willing to supply for terrorism reinsurance in the short run, but the amount is unknown.

Effects on Economic Activity and Mitigation

The effects of TRIA on economic activity are probably positive although difficult to quantify. TRIA supported commercial construction in New York City and other large metropolitan areas during the recovery from 9/11 and also more recently, for projects like Freedom Tower, which was built on the previous site of the World Trade Center. But in general, TRIA probably has had a bigger effect on the location of commercial construction projects than the amount of such construction. In the absence of the federal program, locations outside of major cities would become more attractive. Looking forward, the federal backstop could yield significant benefits by facilitating the economy's recovery in the event of a

---

[52] Assets include cash and securities, as well as property, plant, and equipment, whereas liabilities include benefits payable, reserves for future policy benefits and unpaid losses, and debt. Loss reserves are an accounting estimate of expected losses. However, accepted accounting practices do not require insurers to set aside reserves to cover expected losses from catastrophic events, including terrorist attacks, and the tax treatment of loss reserves discourages them from doing so.

[53] For an overview of the recent financial results, see Property Casualty Insurers Association of America, "P/C Insurers' Net Income Rose Modestly in First-Half 2014 as Increases in Realized Capital Gains Offset Ongoing Weakness in Operating Income" (press release, October 6, 2014), www.pciaa.net/pciwebsite/cms/content/viewpage?sitePageId=39124.

[54] Those estimates are based on insurers' balance sheets, as opposed to market capitalizations of insurance companies, and vary on the basis of which reinsurers are included. For details, see Marsh & McLennan Cos., "Re: Request for Comments on the President's Working Group on Financial Markets: The Long-Term Availability and Affordability of Insurance for Terrorism Risk" (September 16, 2013), pp. 9–10, www.regulations.gov/#!documentDetail;D=TREAS-DO-2013-0003-0027; Guy Carpenter & Company, *Uncertain Future: Evolving Terrorism Risk* (June 2014), p. 18; Guy Carpenter & Company, *Capital Markets: The Reinsurance Evolution Continues* (September 2014), www.guycarp.com/content/dam/guycarp/en/documents/dynamic-content/Capital%20Markets-TheReinsuranceEvolutionContinues.pdf (1,965 KB); and Aon Benfield, "The Aon Benfield Aggregate: Results for the Six Months Ended June 30, 2014," http://bit.ly/aba1h2014 (1,378 KB).

[55] Reinsurance Association of America, "Re: Request for Comments on the President's Working Group on Financial Markets: The Long-Term Availability and Affordability of Insurance for Terrorism Risk" (September 16, 2013), www.regulations.gov/#!documentDetail;D=TREAS-DO-2013-0003-0018.

large future attack. However, a portion of those benefits could be offset if TRIA increases the losses from an attack by reducing the amount of mitigation that policyholders undertake.

Effects on Economic Activity. Assessing TRIA's effects on the recovery from 9/11 is difficult because it is hard to know how the economy—which was also experiencing the effects of the 2001 recession, among other national and regional influences—would have performed in its absence. Before the law was enacted, anecdotal evidence suggested that some large construction projects had been canceled or delayed, in part because of the lack of terrorism coverage. In the months following TRIA's enactment, nationwide retail construction increased, but office construction and employment in the construction industry continued to decline.[56] Labor markets in New York City were also adversely affected by 9/11, but only for about a year; there was little evidence of a lasting effect on the city's employment, according to one study.[57] How much better (or worse) those trends were because of TRIA is unknown. In addition, lawmakers might have enacted other measures in the absence of TRIA.

If another terrorist attack caused large losses—on the order of those from 9/11, or even bigger—TRIA might hasten the economy's recovery. The direct effects would be on insurers: TRIA might reduce the number of insolvent insurers, the extent to which investors take capital out of the insurance industry, the size of temporary spikes in insurance prices, and the number of insurers withdrawing from state workers' compensation markets. In turn, those effects could imply fewer unpaid claims, faster reconstruction, fewer layoffs by businesses facing very large increases in workers' compensation costs, and fewer layoffs and bankruptcies associated with reduced commercial construction.[58] The effects could also extend to credit markets, such as those for commercial mortgage-backed securities: Credit-rating agencies typically require terrorism insurance coverage for loans pooled into such securities, in part to improve the securities' credit rating and liquidity. The probability of terrorist attacks large enough to cause significant disruptions in insurance markets and the broader economy in the absence of TRIA is believed to be low, however.

Effects on Mitigation. The effects of TRIA on mitigation are also difficult to quantify, in part because little information is available. Businesses insured under TRIA may engage in some mitigation if there are cost-effective ways to reduce losses that would not be compensated (or fully compensated) by insurance. But businesses may do less mitigation than they would otherwise and thus realize increased losses in the event of another attack because the unpriced federal reinsurance allows insurers to charge premiums that are lower and less risk sensitive.

Effects of the Changes Made in the 2015 Reauthorization. Because the reauthorization retains the basic structure of the previous TRIA program, its effects will probably be broadly similar. The new program differs from the previous version of TRIA in two key respects:

---

[56] Congressional Budget Office, *Federal Terrorism Reinsurance: An Update* (January 2005), pp. 9–12 and 18, www.cbo.gov/publication/16210. Also see Jeffrey R. Brown and others, "An Empirical Analysis of the Economic Impact of Federal Terrorism Reinsurance," *Journal of Monetary Economics*, vol. 51, no. 5 (July 2004), pp. 861–898, www.sciencedirect.com/science/article/pii/S0304393204000522.

[57] Jason Bram and James Orr, "Taking the Pulse of the New York City Economy," *Current Issues in Economics and Finance*, vol. 12, no. 4 (Federal Reserve Bank of New York, May/June 2006), www.newyorkfed.org/research/current_issues/ci12-4.html.

[58] Faster reconstruction by itself is not likely to have a significant effect on the economy from the national perspective, because nonresidential investment represents a small share of gross domestic product (2.7 percent in 2013) and commercial office construction's share is even smaller (0.7 percent in 2013). But faster reconstruction would also mean some increases in spending on office equipment and furniture. And depending on the nature of the attack and the size of the losses, faster reconstruction may also be associated with sizable gains in the continuity of business operations and the stability of employment income.

- Increases in the copayments shift more liability to the insurance industry for initial payments on losses. That shift gives insurers somewhat greater incentive to charge premiums that reflect policyholders' individual risks, thus giving policyholders somewhat more incentive to adopt mitigation strategies, such as adding safety features to buildings. Consequently, losses from future terrorist attacks and spending on federal aid after an attack may be slightly smaller than under the previous version of TRIA. Higher copayments may also motivate primary insurers to purchase more private reinsurance.[59]

- The higher aggregate retention amount ($29.5 billion in 2015) increases the federal outlays to be recouped after an attack; indeed, raising the retention amount over time to $50 billion might allow the government to recover all of its outlays in almost all cases. However, the taxes required to achieve the recoupment targets after a big attack could be significantly higher than under previous law. In addition, that approach might distort insurance markets by recouping costs from all commercial policyholders, many of whom have limited exposure to terrorism risk.

Policy Options

Prior to TRIA's reauthorization in January 2015, CBO analyzed a variety of options for federal support of terrorism risk insurance. This paper examines in more detail some options that remain alternatives that might be considered in the future:

- Amending TRIA to increase the share of risk borne by insurers—by adjusting private payment amounts in various ways or by limiting what TRIA covers;

- Pricing TRIA coverage to improve mitigation incentives and reduce reliance on recoupments after an attack; and

- Providing tax benefits to stimulate the private provision of terrorism coverage.

CBO evaluated how changes to the current program would affect the availability of private insurance; the amount of risk shifted from the government to private parties; mitigation incentives; demands for assistance after an attack; and the economy (see Table 1). Even though the options are examined on a stand-alone basis, they could also be combined in various ways.

Options to Increase Risk Sharing in TRIA

CBO analyzed a range of options that would reduce federal spending and transfer more risk from the government to private insurers and policyholders.[60] The options could be structured as interim measures before the eventual elimination of TRIA but would also be compatible with a permanent program. Lawmakers could do the following, either in isolation or in various combinations:

---

[59] For one analysis of the distribution of spending under similar program designs, see Howard Kunreuther and others, *TRIA After 2014: Examining Risk Sharing Under Current and Alternative Designs* (The Wharton School, University of Pennsylvania, Summer 2014), http://tinyurl.com/l6sh6vp (PDF, 1,691 KB).

[60] CBO has produced cost estimates for bills that include some provisions that transfer risk. For example, see Congressional Budget Office, cost estimate for S. 2244, Terrorism Risk Insurance Program Reauthorization Act of 2014 (December 9, 2014), www.cbo.gov/publication/49845, cost estimate for S. 2244, Terrorism Risk Insurance Program Reauthorization Act of 2014 (June 24, 2014), www.cbo.gov/publication/45474, and cost estimate for H.R. 4871, TRIA Reform Act of 2014 (July 15, 2014), www.cbo.gov/publication/45535.

Table 1.
Anticipated Effects of Options for Federal Terrorism Risk Insurance

		Effects of Possible Changes to the Current Program			
	Current Program	**Shift Risk From the Government to Private Parties by Adjusting Deductibles, Copayments, Retention Amount, and Program Cap**	**Shift Risk From the Government to Private Parties by Limiting Coverage to NBCR Risks**	**Charge Risk-Based Prices for Federal Reinsurance**	**Change the Tax Code to Encourage Private Insurers to Cover Terrorism Risks**
Availability of Private Insurance	Widely available except for some high-risk properties.	Slightly less available under most versions of the option.	Less available and potentially subject to major disruptions after a big attack, but the availability of workers' compensation insurance would be less affected.	Slightly less available.	Somewhat more available, assuming federal program remains in place.
Risk to Government	If recoupments after an attack occur as specified, the government's risk is limited to its share (85 percent in 2015, decreasing to 80 percent in 2020) of losses above the aggregate retention amount ($29.5 billion in 2015, rising to about $50 billion in 2020).	Lower.	Lower because no explicit risks from conventional terrorist attacks. Exposure to NBCR risk would be largely limited to workers' compensation policies.	Lower because of less or no reliance on recoupments after an attack (which could be reduced, eliminated, or delayed) and because insurers would slightly reduce their use of federal coverage.	Somewhat higher because of the increase in coverage.
Financial Incentives for Businesses and Other Policyholders to Mitigate Risks	Limited because premiums charged by insurers only partially reflect mitigation efforts.	Somewhat stronger because subsidies would be reduced.	Conventional risk: Market pricing strengthens incentives to mitigate risks, as does the decline in coverage. NBCR risks: No change.	Stronger because subsidies to policyholders would be reduced or eliminated.	Slightly weaker because of the increase in coverage.
Demands for Assistance After an Attack	Those who lack insurance or are underinsured might seek assistance.	Slightly higher. Marginal drop in insurance coverage and the higher potential for losses above the cap would raise demand.	Higher because of the decline in insurance coverage.	Slightly higher because of small increases in the number of uninsured properties.	Somewhat lower because of the increase in insurance coverage.
Economic Effects	Program has small benefits before an attack and might help stabilize the economy after a big attack.	Little or no change.	Commercial activity and development could be reduced in high-risk areas or reduced more broadly after a big conventional attack. Might help stabilize the economy after a big NBCR attack.	Little change.	The change in tax treatment could distort the allocation of capital, which might reduce long-term growth.

Source: Congressional Budget Office.

Note: NBCR = nuclear, biological, chemical, and radiological.

- Raise the trigger for federal involvement;

- Raise insurers' deductibles;

- Raise insurers' copayments;

- Raise the industry's aggregate retention amount;

- Lower the program's cap; or

- Limit coverage to NBCR risks.

Relative to the current program, the options would raise costs for policyholders in various ways. Higher triggers, deductibles, and copayments would increase costs to policyholders carrying terrorism insurance because the changes would shift more risk to insurers, which would pass on the cost of that risk through higher premiums for terrorism coverage. Lowering the program's cap would raise costs to those same policyholders, by boosting premiums for supplemental private policies to cover the gap or by increasing policyholders' exposure to terrorism risk. Raising the aggregate retention amount could push up costs to all policyholders carrying property and casualty coverage, in the form of higher assessments after a very costly terrorist attack.

To illustrate a range of possible outcomes, CBO analyzed the potential effects of four options relative to the current program:

- Option 1 would raise insurers' deductibles to 25 percent of prior-year premiums over five years and increase copayments for losses above the deductibles to 25 percent, also over that period. Under current law, copayments are scheduled to increase to 20 percent. Other provisions of the current program, including the scheduled increases in the aggregate retention amount and the liability cap, would remain unchanged under this option.

- Option 2 would raise deductibles and copayments to 30 percent and increase the trigger for federal involvement to $500 million. Those increases also would be phased in over five years.

- Option 3 would immediately lower the program cap to $80 billion but retain the current deductibles, copayments, and retention amount.

- Option 4 would limit TRIA's coverage to losses from NBCR attacks.[61]

Other options not considered here could involve the government's providing more coverage after an attack and less coverage, or none at all, during other periods. (Options of that type have been proposed for the former program that provided terrorism insurance to commercial airlines and for the government's involvement in the secondary mortgage market.)[62]

---

[61]The option analyzed here would not require insurers to offer NBCR coverage, but other analysts have developed options that would. See Dwight Jaffee and Thomas Russell, "Responding to WMD Terrorism Threats: The Role of Insurance Markets," in Stephen M. Maurer, ed., *WMD Terrorism: Science and Policy Choice* (MIT Press, 2009), pp. 251–286, http://mitpress.mit.edu/books/wmd-terrorism.

[62] For example, the Administration had a proposal to limit coverage under the Aviation War Risk Insurance Program (which expired on December 31, 2014) to NBCR risks, albeit with a provision that gave the Secretary of Transportation the authority to include conventional attacks in the program for 90 days after a widespread disruption in the insurance market. See Bart Elias, Rachel Y. Tang, and Baird Webel, *Aviation War Risk Insurance: Background and Options for Congress*, Report for Congress R43715 (Congressional Research Service, September 5, 2014). If the Congress eliminated TRIA entirely, the fact that it had created the program after 9/11 and could take similar action again after a significant future attack could help maintain the current availability of terrorism insurance.

Increasing risk sharing with the private sector is consistent with the improved financial condition of insurers since 2007. For most insurers, potential exposure to losses from a terrorist attack was between 8 percent and 12 percent of their capital in 2014; they generally try to keep that exposure under 20 percent.[63] (Rating agencies would lower the credit ratings of insurers whose terrorism exposure was considered too large.)[64] Changes to TRIA that significantly increased insurers' exposure would lead many to seek more private reinsurance; some spokespeople for the reinsurers have said that their industry is willing to take on more conventional terrorism risk, though not NBCR risk.[65] (NBCR risks are less amenable than conventional attacks to market solutions because of the lack of data on which to base projections and because their costs could be much larger.)

Budgetary Effects. CBO estimated that the options would have the following broad effects on federal spending, measured in expected-value terms, compared with the current program:

- Options 1 and 2 would reduce federal spending modestly, primarily because of their increases in deductibles and copayments. Option 2's increase in the trigger level (to $500 million) would have little effect, because insurers' deductibles, copayments, and recoupments would cover almost all of the budgetary costs from attacks that caused less than $500 million in losses.

- Option 3, which lowers the program's cap to $80 billion, would have negligible effects on spending, for a similar reason: The risk models underlying CBO's estimates attach a very small probability to attacks causing insured losses between $80 billion and $100 billion.

- Option 4, which extends TRIA only for NBCR risks, would narrow the scope of the program and thus reduce expected outlays. In 2014, CBO estimated that expected average annual insured losses from NBCR attacks would be $650 million over the program's lifetime and that the large majority of those losses would be covered by insurers' deductibles and copayments. However, NBCR attacks are slightly more likely than conventional attacks to produce losses that exceed the industry's aggregate retention amount, so some costs might not be recouped.

In general, lower expected federal spending under the above options would mean that the amount of losses to be recouped would be lower, so revenues would also fall. Because the surcharge is 140 percent of the amount of spending to be recouped, which is slightly higher than the rate required to offset revenues lost through lower corporate income and payroll taxes, the net effect could be somewhat lower budgetary savings—or possibly even net costs under Option 4.

This analysis does not account for the budgetary effects of possible increases in demand for disaster assistance from businesses and property owners that do not carry terrorism coverage. Nor does it put a price on the government's risk exposure; doing so would increase the costs associated with the current program and increase the budgetary savings associated with lowering the liability cap. The analysis of

---

[63] Report of the President's Working Group on Financial Markets (April 2014), p. 18.

[64] A.M. Best, "The Treatment of Terrorism Risk in the Rating Evaluation," *A.M. Best Methodology* (draft, October 8, 2013). Exposures will increase somewhat as the copayment increases from 15 percent to 20 percent by 2020.

[65] See testimony of Kean Driscoll, chief executive officer, Validus Re, before the Subcommittee on Housing and Insurance of the House Committee on Financial Services (November 13, 2013), http://financialservices.house.gov/calendar/eventsingle.aspx?EventID=360497; and testimony of Edward B. Ryan, Aon Benfield, Subcommittee on Insurance, Housing, and Community Opportunity of the House Committee on Financial Services (September 11, 2012), http://financialservices.house.gov/calendar/eventsingle.aspx?EventID=307443.

Table 2.
Who Would Pay for Insured Losses of $40 Billion in 2020 Under Current Law and Under Options With Greater Risk Sharing?

(Billions of dollars)

	Current Law	Option 1	Option 2
Scenario Parameters			
Insurers' Deductibles (Percent)	20	25	30
Insurers' Copayments (Percent)	20	25	30
Industry's Aggregate Retention Amount	50	50	50
Allocation of Losses			
Insurers' Deductibles[a]	16	20	24
Insurers' Copayments	4.8	5	4.8
Subtotal, Insurers	20.8	25	28.8
Federal Outlays	19.2	15	11.2
Total	40	40	40
Memorandum:			
Recoupments Collected From Surcharges on All Commercial Policyholders[b]	26.9	21	15.7

Source: Congressional Budget Office.

a. Actual deductibles would depend on which individual insurers experienced losses.

b. Equals 140 percent of the difference between the industry's aggregate retention amount (or insured losses, whichever is smaller) and insurers' payments (deductibles and copayments).

revenues assumes that the recoupment mechanism works as specified in law. But the mechanism has yet to be tested, let alone by a very large attack, and policymakers might be hesitant to tax all commercial policyholders, including those without terrorism insurance, after an attack, especially if the economy was weak.

Effects on Risk Sharing in 2020. The effects of the options on the allocation of terrorism losses can be illustrated by a hypothetical example of an attack that causes $40 billion in insured losses. (For comparison, the September 11 attacks caused losses of $44 billion, in 2014 dollars. Another attack of that size is considered unlikely but is analyzed here for illustrative purposes.) The example posits that the attack occurs in 2020, when changes scheduled to occur under current law will be fully in effect, and that the affected insurers' property and casualty premiums in 2019—the basis on which their 2020 deductibles are calculated—total $80 billion.[66]

Under current law, deductibles (as a share of prior-year premiums) and copayments would be 20 percent in 2020, so insurers' deductibles would cover the first $16 billion in losses and their copayments would

---

[66] For alternative attack scenarios, see Howard Kunreuther and others, *TRIA After 2014: Examining Risk Sharing Under Current and Alternative Designs* (The Wharton School, University of Pennsylvania, Summer 2014).

cover another $4.8 billion (20 percent of the losses between $16 billion and $40 billion; see Table 2).[67] Thus, insurers would be responsible for $20.8 billion of the losses, which would leave the government paying $19.2 billion. The Treasury would then impose taxes (or surcharges) on policyholders to recover $26.9 billion (140 percent of the difference between the $40 billion of insured losses and the $20.8 billion of insurers' total payments).[68]

Under Option 1, insurers' deductibles and copayments in 2020 would be 25 percent, so insurers would pay $4.2 billion more and the government would pay $4.2 billion less. In addition, surcharges on policyholders after the attack would drop by almost $6 billion.

Under Option 2, in which deductibles and copayments would rise to 30 percent by 2020, insurers' payments would be $8 billion higher than under current law, and the government's payments would be $8 billion lower. Surcharges on all commercial policyholders would be about $11 billion lower.

Option 3 would have no effect on risk sharing in this example, because the losses would still be well under the reduced program cap of $80 billion. Option 4 would also leave risk sharing the same as under current law if the losses resulted from an NBCR attack. If the attack used conventional weapons instead, the federal government would have no responsibility for the losses under TRIA, but there might be increased demands for assistance afterward.

Effects on Insurance Markets and the Economy. One general effect of the options to shift risk to insurers and policyholders is that private reinsurers would be likely to play a larger role. That change would spread more of the risk internationally, and insurers would typically pass the costs of the private reinsurance on to policyholders.

The response of private insurers and reinsurers to such a shift in risk would depend on the details.

- Under Options 1 and 2, many insurers, particularly large ones, would continue to offer terrorism coverage to their policyholders; the continuation of the federal backstop would lessen concerns about solvency. Some smaller insurers might stop offering terrorism coverage, however—particularly under Option 2, because raising the trigger to $500 million would leave them with no federal protection for many attacks that would be large relative to their capital.[69]

- Under Option 3, the lower program cap would shift risks onto policyholders from insurers as well as from the government, leaving them with less coverage in the event of an attack that exceeded the cap. However, the lower cap might also induce insurers to offer more coverage under the cap and to decrease their rates.

- If TRIA was narrowed to cover only NBCR attacks (Option 4), primary insurers would have to pay for any private reinsurance they obtain for conventional attacks. As a result, they would probably not be willing to provide as much coverage to policyholders, and the price of conventional terrorism coverage might rise significantly. The reduced availability of insurance

---

[67] CBO estimates that the sum of all insurers' deductibles will be about $50 billion in 2020.

[68] All government outlays would be subject to recoupment, because the insured losses are less than the industry's aggregate retention amount of $50 billion. The net revenues to the government would be about 25 percent lower than the $29.6 billion collected, because policyholders would deduct the recoupment charges from the income used to calculate their income and payroll taxes.

[69] Howard Kunreuther and others, *TRIA After 2014: Examining Risk Sharing Under Current and Alternative Designs* (The Wharton School, University of Pennsylvania, Summer 2014), http://opim.wharton.upenn.edu/risk/library/TRIA-after-2014_full-report_WhartonRiskCenter.pdf (1,691 KB). .

would be likely to have an adverse effect on economic growth; that effect would probably be small in most periods, but it could be significant after a big attack if the supply of insurance recovered more slowly than it would have under current law.

Relatively few policyholders would drop their coverage under the first three options, because any increases in premiums would probably be modest (or even negative, in the case of Option 3), and the demand for terrorism insurance is relatively insensitive to price. Those who continued to purchase terrorism insurance might have slightly greater incentives for mitigation if premiums became more sensitive to location or to other risk factors that could be mitigated. The incentives could be stronger for policyholders who choose to self-insure.

Options to Price Federal Terrorism Coverage

Instead of (or in addition to) increasing the risk sharing in TRIA, lawmakers could reduce the program's cost to taxpayers and its subsidies to policyholders by putting prices on terrorism risk, through premiums charged for TRIA coverage or other mechanisms.[70] The original authorizing legislation did not include premiums, in part because the program was viewed as temporary but also because the Treasury had no particular access to information that would allow it to set premiums on the basis of insurers' risk exposure. Now, the Treasury could consult with the same modeling firms used by private insurers (and perhaps additional governmental analyses).

Specifically, the Treasury could use three approaches to set premiums for TRIA coverage:

- It could set specific dollar rates, based on its determinations of terrorism risk nationally, or of the risks faced by different insurers;

- It could set rates as a share of premiums collected by primary insurers, based on those same determinations; or

- It could purchase private reinsurance to cover a portion of its risks and set its premiums by reference to the price it pays for that reinsurance.

Two other approaches would put a price on terrorism risk without charging premiums for reinsurance.

- One approach would involve changing the nature of TRIA's financial protection from traditional reinsurance to standardized contracts, to be sold by auction.

- The other approach would maintain the current reinsurance coverage and continue to rely on recoupments but would make the amount assessed to policyholders depend on some indicators of each one's exposure to terrorism risk.[71]

Premiums set by the Treasury could depend on legislative choices about the goal of the premiums: to reduce subsidies; to achieve budget neutrality, taking into account the offsetting reductions in income and payroll tax receipts; or to achieve budget neutrality and compensate taxpayers for the program's market risk.[72] For some insurance programs, lawmakers require that premiums be set on an actuarially sound

---

[70] Charging an up-front premium would be compatible with raising deductibles or copayments; it would weaken the argument for surcharges after an attack, however.

[71] In the approaches examined here, rate setting or other pricing of risk is the responsibility of the Treasury. An alternative would be to stipulate premium rates in law.

[72] If premiums were set at market levels and reflected fair values, then taxpayers would be compensated for market risk. For an analysis of the fair-value approach in the context of federal credit programs, see testimony of Douglas W. Elmendorf, Director,

basis—that is, so as to cover expected losses. That guidance generally gives federal administrators considerable flexibility, because estimates of actuarially sound premiums vary and whether to include market risk is ambiguous. Pressure from beneficiaries of insurance programs to keep rates affordable can make actuarial soundness hard to achieve.

An example of a government program that set premiums in dollar terms was the federal Aviation War Risk program, which offered primary terrorism insurance coverage (not reinsurance) from September 2001 to December 2014, when it expired. Under the program, which was narrower in scope than TRIA, the Federal Aviation Administration sold insurance to air carriers and certain manufacturers; the insurance covered liabilities arising from terrorist attacks (including NBCR attacks), hijackings, and some types of vandalism. CBO projected that over the long run the program would have a small expected cost to the government.[73] For example, whereas premiums averaged about $175 million a year from 2003 to 2013, CBO's estimate of annual expected losses, which fell over time, was about $250 million toward the end of that period, implying net budgetary costs of about $75 million for a year's worth of coverage. The main source of the expected losses was the provision that assigned to the federal government liability for terrorism-related damages to third parties in excess of $100 million, regardless of whether the airline purchased the program's insurance. The Federal Aviation Administration was prohibited from raising premiums to cover the program's expected losses because of Congressional directives that the agency must offer the coverage at terms and rates "no less favorable" than those offered in 2002. Nonetheless, because no major attacks occurred during the program's existence (only three relatively small claims were paid out), it ended up running a surplus.

An example of a program that charges insurers a percentage of the premiums they collect for terrorism coverage is the United Kingdom's terrorism risk insurance program. The approach currently taken by that program is that 50 percent of the terrorism premiums collected by a mutual insurance pool for terrorism risk are passed through to the government for its reinsurance backstop program (see the appendix). That approach may be easier to implement because the government does not have to determine premiums, only the appropriate pass-through percentage. In a limited way, the approach uses information produced by market forces: If, for example, the price of terrorism insurance rose—perhaps because the perceived risk of attack increased—the effective price of TRIA's reinsurance would rise as well.

The third approach to setting premiums outlined above, in which the government obtains a more direct measure of the market value of TRIA coverage by paying private reinsurers to accept a share of the government's exposure, is illustrated by the Australian terrorism program (see the appendix). Depending on policymakers' goals for TRIA, those premiums might or might not be set equal to the prices charged by private reinsurers, but the latter prices would at least provide a reference point. Initially, the government might reinsure a small fraction of its exposure; it would not strain the current capacity of the reinsurance market to take on 1 percent or 2 percent of TRIA exposure, for example. The government could increase its purchases over time if private reinsurers were willing to assume more of the risk, as has been true in Australia.

The government would not have to set any prices if it auctioned a standard form of terrorism coverage instead of providing traditional reinsurance. In the event of a terrorist attack that triggered payouts on the contracts, each holder of the same type of contract would receive the same amount—a certain percentage of the total losses of some group of insurers above a collective deductible, for a certain type or location of

Congressional Budget Office, before the House Committee on Financial Services, *Estimates of the Cost of the Credit Programs of the Export-Import Bank* (June 25, 2014), www.cbo.gov/publication/45468.

[73] Congressional Budget Office, cost estimate for H.R. 4986, the National Defense Authorization Act for Fiscal Year 2008 (January 25, 2008), www.cbo.gov/publication/19449.

attack—regardless of the contract holder's own losses.[74] (Standardizing the contracts would help generate interest from multiple bidders, which would be necessary for the sale prices to reflect market valuations of the coverage.) Different contracts could be offered to approximate the exposures of different groups of insurers: Some contracts might pay off based on the losses of smaller insurers from attacks on the West Coast, for example, while others might be based on the losses of midsize businesses from attacks in New York or New Jersey. The total federal exposure would depend on the number of contracts of each type auctioned and the percentage of losses paid by each contract. For example, 60 contracts each paying 1 percent of the specified losses would yield the same federal exposure as 30 contracts each paying 2 percent of those losses. To encourage competition in the bidding and limit the government's exposure, the number of contracts auctioned would need to be rationed. Deciding what contracts to offer and how to auction them would take some time—possibly more than a year.

Under the final approach to introducing some pricing for terrorism risk, the existing system of recoupments after an attack would continue, but it would depend on policyholders' risk levels, determined in part by their experience. Detailed estimates of those risk levels would be desirable in principle, but as a practical matter, the recoupments would probably reflect only broad risk classifications. For example, they could be based on a classification of locations as high risk, moderate risk, or low risk.[75] Experience-based ratings have been used in other federal insurance programs. In the unemployment insurance program, for instance, the premiums that employers pay are partly based on the unemployment compensation paid to their former employees. But such insurance programs have more frequent claims than terrorism insurance and thus a sounder basis for adjusting premiums on the basis of experience. Moreover, past losses from terrorist attacks would not necessarily be indicative of future losses from such attacks.

Budgetary Effects. The budgetary effects of the approaches to put prices on terrorism risk would depend on the specific legislative language used to define the chosen approach, as well as on the Administration's implementation of that language. But the particular issues affecting the different options, and their broad qualitative implications, are discussed below.

For reference, CBO expects that under current law, TRIA's administrators would need to charge average premiums of nearly $600 million per year (for six years) to offset the government's projected losses on a cash basis. However, any premiums paid to the government (or collections from the auctions) would be subject to the same reduction in gross revenue that applies to the surcharges under TRIA—over 25 percent each year—to reflect offsetting effects on income and payroll taxes. Consequently, collections would need to average roughly $800 million a year for the net revenues to offset expected federal outlays over the life of the program. If that amount was collected, CBO projects small expected budgetary savings over the 2015–2024 period, because the premiums would be collected before all the expected claims were paid out.

For the two approaches that would base premiums on administratively determined estimates of terrorism risk, the difficulty of estimating those risks makes it uncertain whether premiums could be set high

---

[74] Similar coverage for natural disasters is discussed in Christopher M. Lewis and Kevin C. Murdock, "The Role of Government Contracts in Discretionary Reinsurance Markets for Natural Disasters," *Journal of Risk and Insurance,* vol. 63, no. 4 (1996), pp. 567–597, www.jstor.org/stable/i302753; and Lewis and Murdock, "Alternative Means of Redistributing Catastrophic Risk in a National Risk-Management System," in Kenneth A. Froot, ed., *The Financing of Catastrophic Risk* (University of Chicago Press, 1999), pp. 51–92, http://papers.nber.org/books/froo99-1.

[75] One rating agency has developed such a classification, grouping U.S. cities into three risk tiers, with five cities in the highest tier, about 20 in the second tier, and all others in the lowest tier. See Thomas M. Mount, Michael Russo, and Andrew Colannino, "The Treatment of Terrorism Risk in the Rating Evaluation," *A.M. Best Methodology* (draft, October 8, 2013), www3.ambest.com/ambv/ratingmethodology/OpenPDF.aspx?rc=217563.

enough to fully offset expected federal insurance payouts or to meet any other stated policy goal. Estimates of expected losses vary, and administrators might choose one of the lower estimates to keep premiums at a level that was deemed affordable. Moreover, if many years passed without an attack, insurers might push for refunds. Thus, either of those approaches could fall short of its policy goal unless it was coupled with ongoing adjustments in premiums to recover past losses, as is essentially the case with the Federal Deposit Insurance Corporation's premiums.

Premiums set using the approach involving the federal purchase of private reinsurance could be subject to some of the same arguments from stakeholders. However, the prices the government paid for that reinsurance would provide information about how private investors see the level of terrorism risk, and that information could help narrow the scope of the arguments.

If TRIA was amended to auction coverage in the form of standardized contracts, the budgetary effects would depend on the value insurers placed on the contracts and the competitiveness of the auctions. If enough contracts were auctioned and insurers were sufficiently risk averse, the auction proceeds could conceivably exceed the expected budgetary costs of the payouts on the contracts and provide some compensation to taxpayers for bearing market risk. One factor making that outcome somewhat less likely, however, is that insurers would tend to pay less for standardized contracts than for traditional reinsurance with the same expected payouts, because the contracts would not compensate perfectly for the losses of individual insurers.

Alternatively, if TRIA was reauthorized and maintained its recoupments but made them more risk sensitive, the budgetary effects would depend not only on the details of the recoupment plan, but also on whether the plan was indeed carried out after attacks that led to federal outlays.

Effects on Insurance Markets and the Economy. In varying ways and to varying degrees, all five approaches to setting premiums for TRIA coverage could give policyholders a more complete price signal of their terrorism risk and thus more financial incentive to mitigate that risk. The approaches that would raise insurers' up-front costs—through premiums for the current TRIA coverage or winning bids for standardized contracts—could do so if insurers passed those costs on to policyholders in ways that were reflective of the policyholders' risks. Such risk-based pricing by insurers might be more likely in the case of premiums for standard reinsurance, particularly to the extent that the reinsurance premiums were sensitive to the risks faced by each insurer's policyholders. Even in the case of auctioned contracts, however, insurers might use risk-based charges to cover the costs of those contracts, especially if they view their purchases of the contracts as driven by the extent of the policyholders' risks. The risk-related recoupments after an attack would be less effective in giving businesses—in this case, all businesses carrying property and casualty insurance—information about their terrorism risk: Businesses might be unaware of the charges until the first time an attack triggered the charges, and the information (and mitigation incentive) conveyed by the charges would be limited by the broad nature of the underlying risk classes. For those reasons, relying on recoupments after an attack would be less effective in providing incentives to mitigate risks than would charging in advance.

Although the demand for terrorism insurance is relatively insensitive to price, if insurers faced up-front costs (for traditional reinsurance or standardized contracts) and raised their premiums to cover those costs, some policyholders—particularly those who underestimated their risks—might drop their coverage. To the extent that take-up rates for terrorism coverage fell, demands for aid after an attack might increase. Moreover, if the increases charged by insurers were not closely related to policyholders' individual risks, adverse selection could occur—that is, the better risks might drop out disproportionately. In the case of traditional reinsurance, adverse selection could have budgetary effects for the government, because it would tend to lead the government to underestimate TRIA's premiums.[76]

A final effect could occur if prices charged for federal reinsurance were sufficiently close to market rates, or if auctions for standardized contracts were sufficiently competitive. In those cases, private suppliers of capital might be able to compete for at least some business—if not now, then in the future.

Options to Change the Tax Code to Encourage Private Insurers to Cover Terrorism Risk

Providing reinsurance is not the only way the federal government could encourage the private supply of terrorism insurance.[77] When TRIA was being designed, the Congress considered changes to the tax code as a way of encouraging private supply. Similar proposals have been made to increase the supply of private insurance for natural disasters.[78]

Taxes by their nature distort some types of business decisions and limit supply, but those distortions are especially severe when it comes to insuring catastrophic risks, such as large terrorist attacks and major natural disasters.[79] The federal tax code and private-sector accounting standards currently discourage property and casualty insurers from setting aside reserves against low-probability risks by not counting additions to those reserves as expenses. (In contrast, reserves for losses that have been reported by policyholders but that remain unsettled are considered expenses, as are reserves for losses that are believed to have already occurred but for which claims have not yet been reported.) Thus, in years in which no terrorism attacks occur, insurers are taxed on their annual premium income, whether or not some of those receipts are set aside for future expected losses. One result is that insurers raise less capital for catastrophic risk than they would otherwise.[80]

Furthermore, the taxation of income on reserves increases the premiums that insurers must charge for terrorism insurance.[81] Taxation of portfolio income is not unique to catastrophe insurance; it is a basic

---

[76] In the case of standardized contracts, adverse selection in purchases of terrorism insurance would not affect the value of the contracts to bid, because the loss threshold that would trigger payouts on the contracts would not be defined in terms of losses to properties carrying terrorism insurance. Issues about take-up rates and adverse selection do not apply to recoupments after at attack, because those are mandatory for all policyholders carrying property and casualty insurance.

[77] Alternative approaches include offering incentives for the mitigation of risk, reducing federal assistance after attacks, and limiting damage awards. To achieve some of the same goals, states could deregulate their insurance markets. See Congressional Budget Office, *Federal Reinsurance for Disasters* (September 2002), pp. 28–33, www.cbo.gov/publication/14008. Another possibility would be for the government to replace TRIA with a policy of lending to insurers following a catastrophic terrorist attack. The government could also intervene in the market for terrorism insurance through direct subsidies to at-risk property and business owners for buying insurance or mitigating risks. See Congressional Budget Office, *Federal Reinsurance for Terrorism Risks: Issues in Reauthorization* (August 2007), pp. 27–28, www.cbo.gov/publication/19035.

[78] For example, see H.R. 2668, the Policyholder Disaster Protection Act of 2005.

[79] David F. Bradford and Kyle D. Long, "The Influence of Income Tax Rules on Insurance Reserves," in Kenneth A. Froot, ed., *The Financing of Catastrophic Risk* (University of Chicago Press, 1999), pp. 275–306, www.nber.org/bookstoc/catastrophetoc.html.

[80] The effects of the taxes are somewhat diminished because insurers are able to deduct the catastrophic losses when they occur. (Deductions in a given year are limited to the amount of taxable income in that year, but with carryforwards and carrybacks, much if not most of the loss would eventually be deducted.) The effects are also somewhat diminished to the extent that insurers buy reinsurance from firms headquartered outside the United States. For various reasons, including informational asymmetries and counterparty risks, insurers do not fully reinsure their catastrophic risks. See Kent Smetters and David Torregrosa, *Financing Losses From Catastrophic Risks*, Working Paper 2008-09 (Congressional Budget Office, November 2008), pp. 12–13, and 19–20, www.cbo.gov/publication/20400.

[81] Scott E. Harrington and Greg Niehaus, "Government Insurance, Tax Policy, and the Affordability and Availability of Catastrophe Insurance," *Journal of Insurance Regulation*, vol. 19, no. 4 (2001), pp. 591–612.

feature of the corporate income tax. But catastrophe insurance is distinguished from other types of insurance by its necessarily high ratio of reserves to expected losses and, therefore, by its high ratio of taxable investment income to expected losses.[82]

One option to change the tax code would be for the government to allow property and casualty insurers to put money aside tax-free to cover expected losses for terrorism risks.[83] A variant of that option would be to also allow income on those reserves to grow free from taxation until the reserves are drawn down. Precedents for alternative treatments of catastrophe reserves exist. Some state-sponsored catastrophe plans, such as those of the Florida Hurricane Catastrophe Fund and the California Earthquake Authority, are structured so that they are exempt from federal and state taxation.[84] Many European countries also allow reserves to be set aside tax-free for catastrophic losses.[85] For example, the mutual reinsurance pool for terrorism risk in the United Kingdom is not taxed on its premium income, which adds to its reserves, although it does pay taxes on its investment income. Moreover, the U.S. federal tax code allows private mortgage insurers, which are required by state laws to set aside 50 percent of their annual premiums in reserves for 10 years to help cover catastrophic losses, to deduct the payments into the reserves, provided that the reserves are invested in special non–interest bearing Treasury bonds with 10-year terms to maturity.[86]

A different option would be to allow insurers to carry back catastrophic losses for 10 or 20 years instead of the current two years for most types of net operating losses, and to recover federal taxes paid in past years. That option also has a precedent: Product liability insurers may carry back losses for 10 years.

In general, changes to the tax treatment of reserves held by property and casualty insurers against expected catastrophic losses would expand the availability of private terrorism risk coverage and lower its costs to policyholders.[87] As a result, the insurance take-up rate might rise slightly, which could lower the demand for assistance after an attack.

Such changes would have several disadvantages, however. First, all the options to change the tax code would affect the timing of revenues and could result in budgetary costs. For example, the option to allow deductions from income for catastrophic reserves would have budgetary costs because it would result in a loss of federal revenue in years without catastrophic losses.[88] If lawmakers extended the same treatment

---

[82] Dwight M. Jaffee and Thomas Russell, "Catastrophe Insurance, Capital Markets, and Uninsurable Risks," *Journal of Risk and Insurance*, vol. 64, no. 2 (1997), pp. 205–230.

[83] Edward B. Rust, Jr. and Kerry Killinger, "The Financial Services Roundtable Blue Ribbon Commission on Mega-Catastrophes: A Call to Action" (Financial Services Roundtable, 2007); and Rawle O. King, *Tax Deductions for Catastrophic Risk Insurance Reserves: Explanation and Economic Analysis*, Report for Congress RL33060 (Congressional Research Service, February 6, 2009).

[84] The Florida fund was established as a tax-exempt state trust fund (State Board of Administration of Florida, Florida Hurricane Catastrophe Fund, Fiscal Year 2012–2013 Annual Report, www.sbafla.com/fhcf/Home/FHCFReports/tabid/315/Default.aspx), and the California authority is considered part of the state government (California Earthquake Authority, Financial Statements December 31, 2013 and 2012, www.earthquakeauthority.com/whoweare/financialstrength/Pages/FinancialStatements.aspx).

[85] Government Accountability Office, *Catastrophe Risk: U.S. and European Approaches to Insure Natural Catastrophe and Terrorism Risks*, GAO-05-199 (February 2005), www.gao.gov/products/GAO-05-199.

[86] If catastrophic losses occur, the bonds are redeemed early and reserves drawn down. Otherwise, the bonds are redeemed after 10 years and the proceeds are taxable. The reserves count as capital.

[87] Congressional Budget Office, *Federal Reinsurance for Disasters* (September 2002), pp. 3–4 and 31–33, www.cbo.gov/publication/14008.

[88] In 2001, the Joint Committee on Taxation estimated that allowing tax-free additions to reserves for terrorism coverage would reduce revenues by more than $12 billion ($15 billion in 2014 dollars) over 10 years. See Congressional Budget Office, cost

to catastrophic reserves for natural disaster risks, the impact on revenues would be even greater. Second, if government oversight was inadequate, insurers could abuse the option to set aside tax-free reserves: By deliberately overestimating expected losses, they could shelter additional income from taxation. That incentive would be stronger if the income on the reserves was also tax-deferred. Deferring taxes on that income would have the additional disadvantage of distorting the allocation of capital between insurers and other financial institutions not subject to the same tax treatment. Such distortions could harm economic growth in the long run.

estimate for H.R. 3210, Terrorism Risk Protection Act as ordered reported by the House Committee on Financial Services (November 16,2001), www.cbo.gov/publication/13394.

Appendix.
Terrorism Insurance Programs in Other Countries

Most developed nations have taken a different approach than that of the Terrorism Risk Insurance Act (TRIA) and instead provide support to terrorism reinsurance pools in return for a share of the premiums collected. Those pools are a way of sharing risks among insurance companies and sometimes with the government. In a pool system, private insurers pay the first layer of claims, and then the reinsurance pools pay the higher layer. Generally, the government picks up the top layer of losses once a pool's resources are exhausted; however, the government may cap its explicit liability. Two programs may be of particular interest to U.S. policymakers. The United Kingdom's Pool Reinsurance Company (Pool Re) is one of the older programs, and it has been tested by multiple terrorist attacks. After the attacks of September 11, 2001, some insurers proposed a similar mutual insurance pool for the United States. Australia's pool is more recent and purchases private reinsurance, which elicits a market price. In both countries, insurers freely set the premiums that their customers pay, as is also the case under TRIA (see Table A-1).

The United Kingdom's Pool Re

More than 20 years ago, the United Kingdom established a government-backed terrorism reinsurance pool—known as Pool Re (for "reinsurance")—to cover property losses from bombings by the Irish Republican Army. Pool Re is mutually owned by participating insurers. Coverage was expanded after the 9/11 attacks to include risks covered by nuclear, biological, chemical, and radiological contamination. Most insurers who offer property and business interruption insurance in the United Kingdom participate in the pool.

Insurers face a relatively small deductible before drawing on Pool Re's reserves. If claims exceed those reserves, the British government pays the rest. The government's obligation is not capped, but its payments must be reimbursed. To date, the pool has not drawn on the government's backstop, though it has paid claims totaling more than £650 million (£1 was $1.53 as of May 27, 2015) from its reserves. By the end of 2014, those reserves had grown to more than £5 billion. In addition, the pool has paid more than £600 million to the government for its backstop.

Pool Re's income comes from premiums and from earnings on invested reserves.[89] Premiums paid to the pool are set as a percentage of insured value, with two different rates for four zones. Rates are highest in central London—0.03 percent of a property's total value—and generally much lower in most other areas outside of central cities.[90] A separate uniform rate applies in all zones for business interruption coverage. In turn, Pool Re pays the government for its unlimited backstop. Before 2015, the pool paid 10 percent of its premiums to the government, but it now pays 50 percent.[91] That increase followed a review of the

---

[89] Pool Re pays no taxes on its premium income but does pay corporate taxes on the investment income earned on its reserves. (Personal communications to the Congressional Budget Office from Greg Dooley of Pool Re, January 31, 2014; February 14, 2014; February 20, 2015; and March 18, 2015.)

[90] Airmic Technical and Willis, *Terrorism Insurance Review 2013* (June 2013), www.willis.com/Client_Solutions/Services/ Political_Risk/Publications/.

[91] Julian Enoizi, chief executive, Pool Re, "Notice of Extraordinary Meeting and Explanatory Letter From the Chief Executive" (November 5, 2014). Premiums (and any dividends—see below) the pool pays to the government would be credited against any future draw on the government's backstop.

Table A-1.
Comparing Features of Terrorism Programs in Australia, the United Kingdom, and the United States

	Australia	United Kingdom	United States
Coverage of Nuclear, Biological, Chemical, and Radiological (NBCR) Risks	Biological and chemical risks covered, if covered by the primary insurance policy, but not nuclear or radiological risks.	Yes.	NBCR covered where it is covered by the primary insurance.
Workers' Compensation Coverage	No.	No.	Yes.
Insurers' Deductibles	Up to $10 million (Australian dollars) for an individual firm and $100 million for all insurers.	£200 million per year (£100 per event) prorated across all participating insurers (though under review by Pool Re).	20 percent of prior year's total premiums in covered lines for an individual firm.
Premiums to Government	Insurers pay premiums to the government's pool, and the pool pays an annual fee plus dividends to the government.	Pool Re pays 50 percent of its premiums to the government.	None, but mandatory recoupment of government payments after an attack for losses under an aggregate retention amount ($29.5 billion in 2015).
Caps on Government's Payments	$10 billion (Australian dollars).	Unlimited.	$100 billion for combined payments by the government and private insurers.
Terrorism Claims to Date	None (The losses from the attack on the Sydney café, which was certified as a terrorist attack, were less than the insurers' deductibles).	Pool Re has paid claims of more than £650 million from 14 attacks without drawing on the British government's backstop.	None (The Boston Marathon bombings resulted in less than $5 million in property and casualty claims and thus were not certified as a terrorist attack under TRIA).

Source: Congressional Budget Office.

Note: As of May 27, 2015, £1 = $1.53 U.S.; $1.00 Australian = $0.77 U.S.; TRIA = Terrorism Risk Insurance Act.

terrorism program by Pool Re and the government and was intended to provide more compensation to taxpayers for the risk they assume.

The review resulted in agreements between Pool Re and the government on a number of policy changes. For example, the pool is now allowed to pay dividends to members and the government as long as it remains profitable.[92]

In addition, the agreement allows Pool Re to set premiums that better reflect the risks, and thus encourage a wider take-up of coverage and more investment in mitigation. For example, the pool plans to set different rates for each of the four zones, as well as specific rates for small businesses outside of London with discounts of up to 40 percent. And it has started offering mitigation discounts (2.5 percent of premiums) to selected properties in London if they meet certain government safety standards. A number of firms offered the discounts have responded by upgrading their security measures, and Pool Re expects that most of the eligible properties will do so. The pool hopes to offer additional inducements for mitigation to a wider range of companies in the future.

In another significant change, the pool purchased private reinsurance for the first time in March 2015—£1.8 billion of coverage from about 30 firms, at a cost of £36 million. Improved risk modeling and greater capacity in the global reinsurance market helped make the purchase attractive.

Australia's Reinsurance Pool Corporation

A global pullback in insurers' willingness to cover terrorism risk after the 9/11 attacks led Australia to establish a reinsurance pool.[93] Under the Terrorism Insurance Act of 2003, insurers are generally not allowed to exclude terrorism losses from coverage; most insurers participate in the government-owned pool, and most commercial properties in Australia are insured by those participants. Coverage includes claims for business interruption, as well as chemical and biological risk (if covered by the primary policy), but excludes workers' compensation and nuclear and radiological risks. To date, one event has been officially declared a terrorist attack—the hostage crisis that occurred in Sydney on December 15, 2014.

A notable feature of Australia's pool is its purchase of private reinsurance, which spreads risk globally and provides a market price signal. Prices for the reinsurance have fallen since the first purchase in 2009, and the pool's purchases have increased. To reduce the pool's exposure to default risk, reinsurance is purchased from multiple sellers in the global marketplace.

Although the reinsurance pool in Australia is government-owned and limits are set on the government's total liability, the Australian program shares some features of the United Kingdom's Pool Re. Different funding layers exist to pay claims; the government's backstop of AUS $10 billion (about $7. 8 billion in U.S. dollars at the exchange rate of $1 AUS to $0.77 U.S. as of May 27, 2015) pays claims only after other sources have been exhausted. (The figures below are in Australian dollars.) Insurers pay a very small first layer of claims; the second layer is paid by the pool, using its reserves; and the next layer ($2.9 billion in 2015) is paid by private reinsurance purchased by the pool along with copayments by the government; remaining losses up to the program's capacity of $13.3 billion in 2015 are covered by the

---

[92] The reinsurance carries a deductible of about £500 million. Personal communication to the Congressional Budget Office from Julian Enoizi, chief executive officer of Pool Re, May 27, 2015.

[93] Commonwealth of Australia, "Terrorism Insurance Act Review: 2012," http://arpc.gov.au/2012/05/31/review-of-the-scheme/.

Australian government.[94] Should losses exceed the program's capacity, the insurance payments to policyholders would be prorated. The Australian Treasury Minister has the option to increase the pool's premiums to recoup losses and repay the government after an attack.

The Australian pool receives a percentage of the premiums charged by private insurers for the underlying insurance policies. The percentage ranges from 2 percent to 12 percent under a three-tiered risk-pricing structure; the highest rates are charged for coverage in the central business districts of Australia's major cities. The rates are set by the Treasury and have not changed since 2003. In the 12 months ending June 30, 2014, the pool collected $130 million in premiums, most of which was used to purchase reinsurance from more than 50 firms, and its reserves exceeded $500 million.[95]

The pool compensates the government for its guarantee.[96] On January 1, 2013, the Australian Reinsurance Pool Corporation began paying "dividends" to the government for its $10 billion backstop for the pool's first eight years. As of June 30, 2014, the pool had paid $325 million. In its May 2014 budget, the Australian government required that the pool pay an annual fee of $55 million for the guarantee, plus a dividend of nearly $60 million for the next four years. (In setting the annual fee payments, the Australian government can use the premium rates that the pool pays for reinsurance as a point of comparison.)

---

[94] Personal communication to the Congressional Budget Office from Michael Pennell, chief underwriting officer, Australian Reinsurance Pool Corporation, March 18, 2015. The attack on the café in Sydney on December 15, 2014, which resulted in two innocent deaths and multiple people taken as hostages, was certified by the government as a "declared terrorist incident." However, the property losses were small (expected losses of about $1.5 million), and the pool expects that those losses will be covered by insurers' deductibles.

[95] Personal communication to the Congressional Budget Office from Christopher Wallace, chief executive officer, Australian Reinsurance Pool Corporation, January 20, 2015. Also see Australian Reinsurance Pool Corporation, *ARPC Annual Report 2013–2014* (September 24, 2014), http://arpc.gov.au/news-and-publications/annual-reports/.

[96] Commonwealth of Australia, "Terrorism Insurance Act Review: 2012," http://arpc.gov.au/2012/05/31/review-of-the-scheme/; and personal communication to the Congressional Budget Office from Michael Pennell, Australian Reinsurance Pool Corporation, September 20, 2013.